# INVOLVING PATIENTS AND THE PUBLIC

## How to do it better

### Second edition

Ruth Chambers, Chris Drinkwater
and Elizabeth Boath

RADCLIFFE MEDICAL PRESS

**Radcliffe Medical Press Ltd**
18 Marcham Road
Abingdon
Oxon OX14 1AA
United Kingdom

**www.radcliffe-oxford.com**

The Radcliffe Medical Press electronic catalogue and online ordering
facility. Direct sales to anywhere in the world.

---

British Library Cataloguing in Publication Data

A catalogue record for this book is available from the British Library.

ISBN 1 85775 994 X

Typeset by Advance Typesetting Ltd, Oxon
Printed and bound by TJ International Ltd, Padstow, Cornwall

# ► CONTENTS

**Ruth Chambers** has been a general practitioner for more than 20 years. Her interest in involving patients and the public in making decisions about healthcare and services has evolved during many development projects across the NHS. The information and tips given in the book have come from personal experience of many of the quantitative and qualitative methods described. She has run focus groups and other types of small group discussions, undertaken many questionnaire surveys delivered by post, telephone, in newspapers or as face-to-face interviews and tried out consensus methods such as the Delphi technique. Ruth is the programme lead for the Teaching PCT in North Staffordshire and Professor of Primary Care Development at Staffordshire University.

Other influences in the thinking behind the contents and direction of the book have been gained from Ruth's time as Chair of Staffordshire Medical Audit Advisory Group, membership of the Royal College of General Practitioners' Council and education lead for the NHS Alliance Executive.

**Chris Drinkwater** has worked as an inner city GP in Newcastle-upon-Tyne for 23 years. Chris is now Professor of Primary Care Development and Head of the Centre for Primary and Community Care Learning at the University of Northumbria. The overall aim of the Centre is to work with the primary and community care services in order to support the development of high quality services, which are sensitive to the needs and expectations of local people.

During the early 1990s Chris led the project group responsible for setting up the West End Health Resource Centre, a prototype healthy living centre which was opened by Tony Blair in 1996. He remains heavily involved in the continuing development of the Centre as company secretary for the charitable trust that runs the building. He was awarded a CBE in 1999 for his role in the development of the Centre and in 2000 he became an Honorary Fellow of the Faculty of Public Health Medicine.

From 1995 to 1998 he was the Sir Roy Griffiths/Age Concern/Prince of Wales/Royal College of General Practitioners Educational Fellow for Older People. He was Vice Chair of the Expert Advisory Group on Models of Primary and Community Care for Older People for the National Service Framework for Older People and he is a member of the National Older People's Care Group Workforce Team. He is Chair of the Health Focus Group for the Newcastle Westgate NDC

Partnership, the Public Health Lead for the NHS Alliance and a member of the Alliance Executive.

**Elizabeth Boath** is the Head of Centre for Health Policy and Practice at Staffordshire University. Liz has a PhD, an honours degree in Psychology, and a Certificate in Teaching and Learning in Higher Education. Over the past decade, she has been involved in designing and facilitating a wide range of educational initiatives, workshops and courses for health professionals and lay people, including the innovative *Consumers as Researchers* training course. Elizabeth's research interests include patient and public involvement, perinatal mental health and teenage pregnancy.

# CHAPTER 1

# Achieving a meaningful dialogue with patients and the general public

You have to be sincere about wanting to involve patients and the public in making decisions about their own care or about local health services for any such exercise to be successful. You cannot expect ordinary people to put forward their views or take part in any discussion if they think that decisions have already been made and the consultation is just a public relations sham. People were talking about making consumer involvement in the NHS a reality in the early 1990s.[1] A decade later and the NHS has changed out of all recognition with the establishment of primary care trusts. New proposals have been put in place to replace community health councils (CHCs) with Patients' Forums (PFs), Patient Advice and Liaison Services (PALS), and Independent Complaints Advisory Services (ICAS).[2] As yet these new structures have had little impact but they underline an increasing drive to make the NHS more responsive to the voice of patients and the public. The acid test will be 'how have these new structures made things better for patients?'

For those working in the NHS having the skills to involve patients and the public is becoming increasingly important. Trust executives and some of those working in health authorities have had some experience of facing public meetings or holding other consultations but many people working in the NHS have no real experience of involving patients or the public in healthcare, over and above their day-to-day interaction with patients.[3]

Involvement may occur at three levels:

(1) for patients and their own care
(2) for patients and the public about the range and quality of health services
(3) in setting priorities and planning and organising service developments.

There is a mounting body of evidence to support the advantages of greater user and public involvement in the NHS.[4–6] The National Consumer

Council cites examples of partnership working between the NHS and users of local health services that have resulted in more efficient use of local community resources, more effective health services and more accountability for public funds.[4] Community development work in Newcastle-upon-Tyne has demonstrated how primary care practitioners come to regard the community as a 'key asset in creating solutions' and become responsive to the community's view.[5] The NHS Executive expect both people's health and healthcare to be improved by participation as in the box below.

---

**The value of greater public participation in the NHS[6]**

*Benefits to the NHS*
▶ Restoration of public confidence.
▶ Improved outcomes for individual patients.
▶ More appropriate use of health services.
▶ Potential for greater cost effectiveness.
▶ Contribution to problem resolution.
▶ Sharing with the public responsibilities for healthcare.

*Benefits to people*
▶ Better outcomes of treatment and care.
▶ An enhanced sense of self-esteem and capacity to control their own lives.
▶ A more satisfying experience of using health services.
▶ More accessible, sensitive and responsive health services.
▶ Improved health.
▶ A greater sense of ownership of the NHS.

*Benefits to public health*
▶ Reduction in health inequalities.
▶ Improved health.
▶ Greater understanding of the links between health and the circumstances in which people live their lives.
▶ More healthy environmental, social and economic policies.

*Benefits to communities and to society as a whole*
▶ Improved social cohesion.
▶ A healthier democracy – reducing the democratic deficit.
▶ A health service better able to meet the needs of citizens.
▶ More attention to crosscutting policy issues and closer co-operation between agencies with a role to play in health improvement.

---

Successive NHS documents have emphasised a vision of a changed culture and practice where user involvement and public engagement are integral to all NHS activities and accountability to the public is more explicit.[7–10] The NHS is becoming more customer focused, where the 'customer' is taken as meaning a patient or user, a carer of a patient, a group of patients or people with similar characteristics or the general public. Involving people in planning services and making decisions about local healthcare does increase their ownership of the NHS and gives them more understanding of how the NHS operates and the problems it faces. Closeness to the customer is reckoned to be a key characteristic of an effective organisation.

---

**The NHS Executive vision**

'The needs of the patient not the needs of the institutions will be at the heart of the new NHS'[7]

'... making sure that the NHS responds more quickly to patients' needs'[8]

'... rebuild public confidence in the NHS as a public service, accountable to patients, open to the public and shaped by their views'[7]

'... ensure that consumer involvement in the NHS R & D pro-gramme improves the way research is prioritised, commissioned and disseminated'[9]

'... patients and carers need to be involved ... in their own care and in the planning, monitoring and development of health services'[8]

'From 1 January 2003, NHS trusts, primary care trusts and strategic health authorities have a statutory duty to involve and consult the public'.[10]

---

There have been some good examples of patient and public involvement where substantial changes have arisen as a result of health authorities consulting local people about the direction of future plans, contracts and services. But many other consultations have been of dubious quality and not been sustained. Some of the reasons for this are thought to be that:

▶ many public engagement initiatives are really public relations exercises in disguise
▶ methods of consultation may be dependent on practitioners' and commissioners' preferences and limited capabilities rather than being the best method(s) for the aim(s) of a particular consultation so that the results are not as meaningful as they might be
▶ there may be a lack of commitment from the consulting organisation or healthcare unit to act on the views obtained

▶ unwanted results may be disbelieved as being unrepresentative of the subject population and ignored
▶ decision making may be based on the historical background rather than a needs assessment or true consultation
▶ public consultation exercises are usually time consuming
▶ the enthusiasm of the response from the public and breadth and detail of information they volunteer sometimes catch the organiser of the consultation unawares and they become overwhelmed.

Other barriers to consultation in general include a lack of funds and a lack of clarity about how to get good public representation. Individuals' lack of confidence, time, training and skills are some of the barriers which deter ordinary citizens from joining in discussions about the health service on equal terms. People are more likely to become involved if they have spare time, for altruistic reasons, because of a personal interest or experience or because they feel strongly about an issue, either being angry about a situation or delighted about the service they have received.

One study of primary care trusts in Liverpool found that neither professionals nor the public were committed to direct public involvement.[11] The author identified the need for a cultural shift to change lay people's attitudes to be more directly involved in decision making rather than merely asking questions and feeding information back to the public.

Meaningful consultation is still in its infancy: precisely which patients and members of the public should be involved in which way, when and to what extent is still the subject of much debate.[12] The evolution of an audit culture in the NHS in the 1990s did encourage a focus on monitoring the quality of care[13] provided, but most such work involved looking at quality from the professionals' perspective rather than that of the users or non-users. In the early 1990s patient satisfaction surveys became the vogue, often focusing on hospitality elements of healthcare services, and involving those who were able and motivated to answer self-completion questionnaires. Although the NHS workforce is unused to involving patients and the public in decision making, others in social services, voluntary organisations or local government are not and have been developing their expertise for years. Learning from their experience should help to avoid wasting time organising meaningless consultations.

If an exercise is to be meaningful, it has to involve people who represent the section of the population that the consultation is about. It is not sufficient to just talk to people who are the pillars of the community who attend everything. You must find ways to seek out the opinions of ordinary people who haven't got time to go to meetings or the inclination to fill in survey forms. People in hard-to-reach groups such as the homeless or those who speak little or no English will be most unlikely to come forward and give their views unless you use an intermediary.

Many consultations at present involve the most accessible people and simply mirror the power balance that already exists in society. Some of the most accessible are voluntary organisations or users' groups; their opinions are not necessarily representative either of the constituents or communities with whom they work. Although their views are important, a range of other opinions are needed if the consultation is to be more than a token activity. You will have to set up systems to actively seek out and involve people from minority groups or those with sensory impairments such as blind or deaf people. And if you do manage to reach individuals in minority groups, don't get to know them too well or use them too often, as your relationship with them will become too close and cosy and they will no longer be truly representative of their sort of people.

Real consultation involves a shift of power. Many of those in trusts or general practices may not be ready for that. Until they are, any user or public involvement in decision making will be a token event. Moving to meaningful user or public involvement will not happen until there is a change in culture where those in the NHS want to engage with people and respond to their views. It is still common for doctors and nurses to assume that they know what is in patients' best interests without asking them and that their own views can be taken as a proxy for those of their patients and the general public. The public will be more likely to perceive a consultation as being genuine if all stages are transparent: the purpose is clear, everyone participating is well informed, all information about the issues is brought out and there are no hidden agendas. One way to ensure that everyone can participate is to minimise the use of jargon and speak and write any public documents in plain English, whether this is about an individual patient's care or management or strategy documents that relate to the local community. If people feel that their opinions matter and their views are valued and incorporated in the decisions that are made they will be more likely to co-operate again in the future.

Consultation takes considerable time, because of the need to use several approaches to find and involve people who are representative of the section of the population that the consultation is all about and gain their trust. The majority of the costs of a consultation are due to the amount of *time* people spend planning the exercise, seeking people out, carrying out the survey or organising interviews, group discussions or public meetings. As well as these direct costs, there are the opportunity costs of the other work they might have been doing. The amount of money or time spent is not necessarily directly proportional to how meaningful the consultation is. Much money can be spent on distributing glossy pamphlets or holding high-profile events like citizens' juries. There may be simpler ways of gaining information, such as asking different groups of people already meeting in clubs or at clinics to comment on the services provided. Ordinary people often have good ideas about saving money and time, having witnessed inefficiencies whilst receiving healthcare. You may not need to invent new, potentially

▼

**True representation?**

costly methods of gaining patients' or the public's views but instead extend some of the ways that already exist. There will also be a need to work closely with the emerging PFs who are responsible for representing the views of local communities to trusts. Professionals and lay people want public involvement to ensure that healthcare is designed and operated for patients, so that the NHS is more responsive to the priorities and needs of the sick. Protocols designed to improve patient care by people who are delivering care across a department or as part of a clinical network, should involve team members as well as patients and users in the process of the development of the protocol. A national resource[14] suggests that information could come from:

▶ patient representatives on the protocol development team
▶ consumer or interest group representatives on the protocol development team
▶ PFs and PALS
▶ patient associations
▶ complaints
▶ analysis of patient and user feedback – both positive and negative.

Although extensive consultation is costly it might be more expensive in the long run not to consult and to continue to waste resources on inappropriate NHS services.

It would not do for staff's views to be overlooked in the rush to consult patients and the public. At the same time as there has been increasing recognition of the need to involve patients and the public, there has been an increasing emphasis on the need to involve and empower frontline staff.[10] *Shifting the Balance of Power*[15] within the NHS recognises that NHS leaders and managers have often neglected to consult staff in the past and consequently unrealistic decisions have been taken that might have been avoided if staff had been involved throughout and their opinions taken into account. Proposals are in place to build staff involvement into objectives for managers and into the performance monitoring arrangements for the NHS.

Closer working between health and social care should mean that patient and public involvement exercises can be co-ordinated with shared action in response. A review of public involvement in six primary care organisations has emphasised the importance of working with other organisations across health economies.[16] Expertise, knowledge and resources can be shared and duplication avoided – but such joint working takes time, effort and patience. Staff should also be involved in a meaningful way in any decision making. They will be as much affected by any changes or improvement programmes as the patients or the public will be. NHS leaders and managers have often neglected to consult staff in the past and consequently unrealistic decisions have been taken that might have been avoided if staff had been properly involved throughout and their opinions taken into account.

Establishing a more positive culture of user involvement and public engagement will require PCTs and other trusts to win the hearts and minds of NHS staff to gain their commitment to really trying to involve patients and the public. That means taking their views into account and not just listening to them. And equally, PCTs and other trusts should understand what motivates lay people (citizens, users and non-users) to become involved in the planning, provision and decision-making processes of primary healthcare and how they can be helped to contribute. This area of work will overlap with the responsibilities of those leading the trust on clinical governance and education and training matters. If services are to be shaped to patients' and the local communities' views, trusts and strategic health authorities will have to develop methodologically sound ways of obtaining such views and encouraging local people and health professionals to participate.

## Involving patients and the public in training NHS staff

The NHS University have published a report that highlights the specific expectations that patients and users have of the NHS and its staff.[17]

These expectations will influence the training themes that the NHS University develops for NHS staff and will include:

▶ empathy and understanding for patients as individuals
▶ the provision of effective information to patients: by all taking the time to provide information that is consistent and accurate, written in a user-friendly way, and given at a time when people are ready for it
▶ the use of patient organisations in providing support: for NHS staff to understand the role and functions of such organisations and involve patient organisations in training
▶ acknowledging and incorporating feedback from patients
▶ a more patient-centred NHS: by staff involving users and carers in all decision making aspects of care, explaining and offering choices.

**Sustained public involvement**

A sustained public involvement programme in a trust will require corporate commitment, leadership, significant resources and a clear strategy.[16] Enthusiasm will be fuelled by positive improvements to patient care and the operating of the trust resulting from public involvement activities. Public involvement that works will be integral to learning and change and connect in some way to the organisation's existing interests. The ceaseless re-organisation of the NHS has inhibited public involvement which requires continuity and stability that give relationships and communications systems opportunities to prosper.

## References

1 Joule N (1993) Involving users of health care services: moving beyond lip service (editorial). *Quality in Health Care*. **2**: 211–12.

2 Department of Health (2001) Involving Patients and the Public in Healthcare: a discussion document. Department of Health, London.

3 Macleod N, Moloney R and Chambers R (1999) *The Education and Training Needs of Primary Care Groups: supporting staff to meet the needs*. Staffordshire University, Stafford.

4 National Consumer Council (1995) *In Partnership with Patients*. National Consumer Council, London.

5 Crowley P (1998) *Involving the community in primary care groups*. Abstract of presentation given at NHS Alliance National Conference, Blackpool. Contact address: West End Health Resource Centre, Adelaide Terrace, Newcastle upon Tyne NE4 8BE.

6 NHS Executive (1998) *In the Public Interest: developing a strategy for public participation in the NHS*. Department of Health, London.

7 NHS Executive (1997) *The New NHS: modern, dependable*. Department of Health, London.

8   NHS Executive (1996) *Patient Partnership: building a collaborative strategy.* Department of Health, Leeds.

9   NHS Executive (1998) *Research: what's in it for consumers?* Department of Health, London.

10  Department of Health (2001) Health & Social Care Act, Section 11. Department of Health, London.

11  Litva A (2003) *Public Involvement in the Quality of Healthcare Services.* Department of Primary Care, University of Liverpool, Liverpool.

12  Renn O, Webler T and Wiedemann P (1995) *Fairness and Competence in Citizen Participation.* Kluwer Academic, London.

13  Kelson M (1998) *Promoting Patient Involvement in Clinical Audit.* College of Health, London.

14  Modernisation Agency and National Institute of Clinical Excellence (2002) *Protocol-Based Care.* NHS Executive, London.

15  Department of Health (2001) *Shifting the Balance of Power.* Department of Health, London.

16  Anderson W, Florin D, Gillam S and Mountford L (2002) *Every Voice Counts. Primary care organisations and public involvement.* King's Fund, London.

17  Sheldon H and Kelly B (2002) *Patient and Service User Priorities for an NHS University Induction Programme.* College of Health, London.

# CHAPTER 2

# Patient and public involvement in the new NHS

The events in the Bristol Children's Cardiac Surgery Unit between 1984 and 1995 and the subsequent public inquiry[1] characterise the changing nature of the relationship between patients, the public and the NHS. This inquiry into a number of avoidable deaths focused on issues of professional accountability and governance and the nature of the partnership between healthcare professionals, patients and the public.

The report of the inquiry chaired by Professor Ian Kennedy produced a total of 198 recommendations grouped under the following categories:

► Respect and honesty.
► A health service which is well led.
► Competent healthcare professionals.
► The safety of care.
► Care of an appropriate standard.
► Public involvement through empowerment.
► The care of children.

Recommendations relating to patient and public involvement included:

► In a patient-centred healthcare service patients must be involved, wherever possible, in decisions about their treatment and care (Rec. 1).
► The education and training of all healthcare professionals should be imbued with the idea of partnership between the healthcare professional and the patient (Rec. 2).
► The notion of partnership between the healthcare professional and the patient, whereby the patient and the professional meet as equals with different expertise, must be adopted by healthcare professionals in all parts of the NHS, including healthcare professionals in hospitals (Rec. 3).
► Patients should receive a copy of any letter written about their care or treatment by one healthcare professional to another (Rec. 17).
► The involvement of the public in the NHS must be embedded in its structures: the perspectives of patients and the public must be taken

into account wherever decisions affecting the provision of healthcare are made (Rec. 157).

▶ The process for involving patients and the public in the NHS must be transparent and open to scrutiny: the annual report of every organisation in the NHS should include a section setting out how the public has been involved, and the effect of that involvement (Rec. 159).

These farsighted recommendations give a flavour of the report but they also make it clear that the report was much more about looking at NHS systems and why they failed parents and children at Bristol, than it was about apportioning individual blame for what went wrong. Recognition of this fact has been one of the main drivers for the wholesale review of systems for patient and public involvement, including consultation papers,[2] abolition of Community Health Councils and amendments to the NHS Act.

Essentially the proposed new structures operate at three different but linked levels: national representation and standards; working in communities and trusts; helping individuals.

## National representation and standards

The Commission for Patient and Public Involvement in Health (CPPIH) established in January 2003 is an independent statutory body which will oversee local Patients' Forums (PFs) in all of the 600 plus hospital, ambulance and primary care trusts in England. At national level there will be a three-way partnership between the Department of Health and elected scrutiny through the parliamentary Health Select Committee. The CPPIH will also employ the local teams which will promote and facilitate involving the public in local decisions through PFs.

The functions of the CPPIH[3] will be:

▶ to identify and disseminate quality standards for the establishment, operation and evaluation of the patient and public involvement system

▶ to develop quality standards for the delivery of Patient Advice and Liaison Services (PALS) and Independent Complaints Advocacy Services (ICAS)

▶ to provide best practice advice to patient and public involvement bodies on recruitment, training, and involvement and engagement processes

▶ to develop best practice guidance on the means of developing capacity within communities to voice their needs and concerns about matters affecting their health

▶ to set out accountability arrangements and minimum professional standards for the services provided by its local network staff

▶ to develop and license training and induction materials for being a patient/public representative in the new system
▶ to undertake and/or commission research on relevant subjects. For example, innovative approaches for involving people from hard-to-reach groups, learning from international experience of patient and public involvement
▶ drawing on sources from its local networks and outreach teams, PALS, local authority, Overview and Scrutiny Committees (OSCs) and PFs, to monitor services nationally from the perspective of patient safety and welfare, and to publish an annual report of its findings, bringing them to the attention of the Secretary of State, the Commission for Healthcare Audit and Inspection (CHAI), the Professional Regulatory Bodies, the National Patient Safety Agency (NPSA) and the Health Select Committee
▶ drawing on views taken from patients and patient organisations, to evaluate the effectiveness of the new arrangements for patient and public involvement and to recommend improvements.

## Working in communities and trusts

At the local level PFs will be established in all NHS Trusts. These PFs will be supported by CPPIH local outreach teams and they will work together in 'federations' within each Strategic Health Authority (SHA). Mirroring the national level where CPPIH links to the Health Select Committee, PFs will link to local authority OSCs. The functions of PFs will be:

▶ to represent the views of local communities to trusts about the quality and configuration of health services. This representation will not be by proxy, but by actively engaging in the community to find out what patients, carers and families think
▶ to monitor service delivery from the patient's perspective, drawing on sources from PALS and the Commission's local networks as well as the formal complaints system, and to examine delivery of change following complaints and work with the trust to bring about improvements
▶ to inspect every aspect of care used by NHS patients from the perspective of the patient's experience of services. This will include new powers to inspect primary care and GP premises and NHS care provided by the independent sector
▶ to produce an annual report of its work and make its findings and reports available not only to trusts, but also to:
  – OSCs
  – local MPs
  – SHAs

- the CPPIH
- the CHAI
- the NPSA, where adverse incidents are concerned.

These reports may be published as part of the trust's annual Patient Prospectus

▶ to elect one of their members to sit as non-executive director on the trust board. It would be good for OSCs to also invite a PF member to join their health scrutiny panels
▶ to monitor the quality of the PALS in the area, and to bring problems to the attention of the trust and the CPPIH against nationally agreed criteria
▶ to monitor the quality of the ICAS in the area (in the case of PFs in primary care trusts) and to bring problems to the attention of the CPPIH.

The other key element at this level is elected scrutiny through local authority OSCs. The Health and Social Care Act 2001 provides specific powers for these committees to look at local NHS provision as part of their wider role in health improvement and reducing health inequalities for their area and its inhabitants. They will do this by gathering evidence and by making routine reports and recommendations to their NHS counterparts. They will be assisted in their work by the Commission's local networks, which will act as a key source of information about the health needs of the local population. There is also provision for these committees to come together to jointly scrutinise cross-boundary services within an SHA area.

---

**GPs' involvement with Patients' Forums**[4]

A primary care trust (PCT) that set up a shadow PF found that there was a great deal of enthusiasm from the local community and GPs. They were able to establish good communication between the trust, GPs and the members of the PF. The GPs' role in involving the public included:

▶ building commitment for the PF through workshops, presentations and written briefings
▶ inviting people to participate in a PF
▶ advertising for local citizens to join the forum – they attracted 'ordinary' NHS users and carers
▶ arranging orientation sessions for potential volunteers
▶ developing agreed terms of reference and protocols between the PCT and PF
▶ providing ongoing training and support for forum representatives, including regular newsletters and learning circles.

Apart from PFs the other key element at local level is the CPPIH's local networks, which are intended to have outreach workers across every PCT area, working from readily accessible community-based premises. These outreach workers will be responsible for commissioning ICAS, providing administrative support for PFs locally and providing a link to local authority OSCs. In addition they will also be expected to build capacity among communities, so that patient and public involvement is constantly improved and strengthened, and to link to local authority work and other activity in the community, which addresses the wider determinants of health. The full set of responsibilities outlined in the Department of Health's response to the listening exercise on public and patient involvement[3] is given below.

▶ Helping to develop the ability of citizens and communities to take greater control of decisions and the organisations and services that affect their health.
▶ Commissioning ICAS for patients, carers or families who need independent support in making a complaint.
▶ Monitoring the quality of complaints handling from the patient's perspective, drawing on information provided by PFs, as well as their experience of the system through commissioning ICAS, to inform them in influencing the development of healthcare locally.
▶ Providing administrative and secretarial support for PFs in their area.
▶ Networking PFs and supporting them in their activities to seek community views on healthcare services.
▶ Providing a means of linking healthcare strategies into wider health agendas, both through panel membership from Local Strategic Partnerships and by providing a link between the role of patient and public involvement and the local scrutiny function by facilitating the sharing of information on critical and strategic issues to OSCs to inform the scrutiny agenda.
▶ Supporting the partners at strategic level and providing a means of channelling information to SHAs to influence wider decisions of long-term configuration and provision of services across the SHA area.
▶ Channelling information to the Commission centrally, to inform its reports and recommendations on nationwide trends and concerns about patient safety and welfare.

In the words of the Department of Health,[3] 'The Commission's local networks are therefore the "glue" which binds together all the arrangements at a local level, acting as a resource both for each new representative body, and for individual patients and communities. In this respect, the local networks and their outreach workers build on the best elements of Community Health Council work on complaints advocacy and on action within communities. The new arrangements go further, being supplemented by all the other complementary components that the networks bring together.'

# Helping individuals

The two new services designed to help patients, carers and families are Patient Advice and Liaison Services (PALS) and Independent Complaints Advocacy Services (ICAS). PALS will have a customer services function and where possible they will resolve problems and concerns before they become formal complaints, ICAS will provide support to people who wish to make a formal complaint.

## *Patient Advice and Liaison Services*

PALS have the following important functions:

▶ To provide information to patients, carers and families, about health and health services locally and put patients in contact with relevant voluntary organisations and support groups.
▶ Where possible, to resolve problems and concerns quickly, before they become more serious.
▶ To inform people of the complaints procedure, and put them in touch with specialist, independent advocacy services when they wish to complain formally.
▶ To act as an early warning system for trusts and PFs, by monitoring problems arising, highlighting gaps in services and staff training, and submitting anonymised reports for action by trusts and PFs.
▶ To operate in a network with other PALS in their area, to ensure a seamless service for patients who move between and use many different parts of the care system for the care they need.

## *Independent Complaints Advocacy Services*

ICAS will support people who want to complain by helping them to articulate their concerns and navigate the complaints system, thereby maximising the chances of their complaint being resolved more quickly and effectively. The commissioning of ICAS will be the responsibility of the CPPIH who will commission ICAS so that it complements existing providers such as the current mental health advocacy service. The CPPIH will also be expected to promote the availability of the service so that people will be able to get support from ICAS providers direct, through the Commission's local networks, as well as via PALS.

# Summary

It can be seen from this brief description of the new arrangements for patient and public involvement that the agenda is enormous. Concerns have already been expressed that the time taken for the re-organisation and the building of new systems has created a vacuum in public and patient involvement and that the attempt to join up all the elements has resulted in a very complex system. There are also very real concerns that the CPPIH will struggle to recruit sufficient people willing to give the time, energy and enthusiasm to over 600 PFs. And from a health-care professional perspective there is a concern that the focus on the need for the CPPIH to be independent has not been balanced by an equal emphasis on the need to develop a systematic approach to ensuring that the views of patients and the public influence the quality of services provided by front line professionals – an issue clearly identified in the Bristol Inquiry Report.[1]

New methods for improving the engagement between healthcare professionals and patients and the public are emerging all the time. There is evidence that professionals need to be empowered to work effectively with the public[5] and that systematic approaches are required. Some of the more promising approaches include Critical Friends Groups and Patients as Teachers.

## Critical Friends Groups[6]

Critical Friends Groups have been piloted in the south west of England. They involve the use of systematic patient feedback questionnaires about a general practice's services, from 50 patients per practitioner. There is increasing evidence that practices using this approach value the input and that it also has an impact on the quality of care provided.[7,8]

## Patients as Teachers[9]

Patients as Teachers is an approach developed in London which adopts a two-stage approach to developing user-centred outcome measures. In the first stage users define good practice from their perspectives and in the second stage they are provided with support to teach these recommendations to professionals. Initial evidence suggests that this approach can be effective in changing behaviour. In addition, these lay defined outcomes can be audited as part of clinical governance arrangements.

For health professionals in the NHS, there is an increasingly important need to understand the new systems for enabling a better informed public to make choices about their own treatment and to get more involved in NHS decision making processes with the aim of making services more responsive and accountable to the public. Within developed societies the evidence is that this is an international phenomenon and that the challenge to medical paternalism is not going to go away.

## References

1   Kennedy I (chair) (2001) *Learning from Bristol: The Department of Health's response to the report of the public inquiry into children's heart surgery at the Bristol Royal Infirmary 1984–1995.* The Stationery Office, London.

2   Department of Health (2001) *Involving Patients and the Public in Healthcare: a discussion document.* Department of Health, London.

3   Department of Health (2002) *Involving Patients and the Public in Healthcare: response to the listening exercise.* Department of Health, London.

4   Brittain I, Taylor B and Tyler S (2002) Contributory factors. *Heath Service J.* **2 May**: 30–1.

5   Pietroni P, Graham L and Winkler F (2001) *Preparing Professionals for Partnership with the Public.* Regional Education Support Unit, NHS London Regional Office, London.

6   Greco M and Carter M (2001) *Establishing Critical Friends Groups in General Practice.* Report to the North East Devon Health Authority. Exeter and North Devon NHS Research & Development Support Unit, University of Exeter, Exeter.

7   Carter M and Greco M (2001) Measuring performance in general practice. *Brit J Gen Pract.* **51**: 847–8.

8   Greco M (2000) Assessing the quality of communications using patient feedback. *Clinical Governance Bulletin.* **3**: 4–5.

9   Fisher B and Gilbert D (2001) Patient involvement and clinical effectiveness. In: *New Beginnings.* Kings Fund, London.

# CHAPTER 3

# Using questionnaire and interview surveys to gather information and views from patients and the general public

You should be sure of your purpose before involving patients and the public in planning and delivering care, know how to choose the right method and how to use the information gained to best effect. Different techniques may give dissimilar results if the methods used are biased. Biases may arise if the sampling of the population is unscientific and the people involved are not representative of the population as a whole, if the questions used are ambiguous or if those participating do not give honest answers. If the consultation is about complex issues like rationing or prioritising healthcare, the participants are likely to need to be informed about the topic first and have opportunities to discuss, debate and reflect on the issues.[1]

This chapter will describe a range of different types of patient or public exercises and some of the advantages and disadvantages of each method. Some methods are more time consuming and costly than others but the outcomes might be more representative of what the general population think. To some extent, there is a trade-off between a method of convenience, which is usually cheaper in terms of resources and maybe more likely to produce biased views, and one where more complex and time-consuming methods are designed to elicit representative opinions from a cross-section of the relevant population. The details given in the boxes of examples not only illustrate the different methods but also provide additional information about how they work in practice. So you should read through the accounts of how the methods have been employed to get a better understanding of how you can apply the variety of methods in the real world.

These methods are not either/or. You will see that they all have different advantages and drawbacks and using one on its own is unlikely to give a full picture of views about the topic in question. The solution is to use more than one method to gauge patient or public opinion and validate your findings.

# Questionnaire surveys

*Good practice with questionnaires in general*

Questionnaires are often used by first-time researchers as the tool of choice for finding out the answer to their research questions. They may mistakenly believe that undertaking a questionnaire survey is one of the simplest and easiest methods. Unfortunately for them, using a questionnaire is full of pitfalls and it is one of the most difficult techniques for gaining a true or valid answer to the question posed.

**The questions**

A valid questionnaire will have questions that:

► are relevant and appropriate to the purpose of the enquiry
► are unambiguous
► contain one idea or enquiry at a time
► have an easily answered format with simple choices of response
► flow in a logical order
► don't make assumptions
► use appropriate language likely to be understood by all respondents
► are not biased or leading
► are not offensive.

You should avoid leading questions that imply that you are expecting a particular answer. Otherwise respondents will tend to give the answer implied as being the 'right' one because they want to please the researcher or because they feel that their own view might be considered to be 'wrong' by others.

Use simple English easily understandable to a typical person in the population you are targeting with the survey. If any words are ambiguous or vaguely descriptive you should either omit them from your question or justify what you mean by them. If any of these kinds of word do slip through, they should be identified by the people in the pilot phase of the study. Don't use jargon. Avoid long and complicated questions.

Only ask questions that people can answer. You do not want people to have to go away to hunt out the answers as they are unlikely to return to complete the questionnaire and your response rate will be low. Similarly, avoid hypothetical questions as far as you can; it is well known that people do not necessarily behave how they say they will in advance of a situation occurring. If respondents have to guess the answers, your responses will be relatively meaningless, so only ask questions to which you can expect accurate answers. If respondents will not be able to answer the questions easily and accurately, choose a different study method.

Be careful not to ask two questions at the same time. This is a very common mistake. You will not know to which part of the double question the answer applies when you are analysing the answers. That's if the subject does reply, as people will be more likely to throw a badly constructed questionnaire away without completing it.

## The answers

It is better to avoid using 'banded' answers in your questionnaire and ask for specific information instead. If your choice of banding is poor you will lose a lot of information if you find that most of your respondents are in one category; for instance, if you were to ask respondents' age as age bands instead of exact years, you might find that 95% were in the age group 30 to 50 years and you would not be able to make any conclusions about the influence of age on the responses they gave. You can always band answers yourself in the analysis stage. But you might purposely choose banded alternative answers for sensitive information such as personal income.

The types of answer will depend to some extent upon whether the questions posed are closed or open ones. The differences and relative advantages between open and closed questions are shown in the box. Closed questions give you a limited choice of options for response; for example, the range of answers to: 'How many times did you ring the surgery before you got through to make this appointment?' might be: once, twice, three or more times. An open question on the same topic might ask: 'Have you experienced any difficulties in phoning into the surgery to make an appointment?' and respondents might give more information about the time of day when there was most difficulty as well as the number of times the phone was usually engaged or the reception they received once the phone was answered. This richness of information is good if you wanted that information but wasteful if your open question triggers unnecessary information that is outside the purpose of your enquiry.

If you ask questions to elicit people's opinions rather than factual information, you might ask for answers using the Likert Scale, a visual analogue scale or the alternative faces type of response as illustrated in the box. Or you might present the respondents with a list of statements from which they can choose the one nearest to their way of thinking.

For the results to be valid and accurate, the respondents must be representative of the target population. The response rate should be high and as near to 100% as possible.

**Drawbacks and benefits of open and closed questions**

| Feature | Open | Closed |
|---|---|---|
| Information content | Potential to be more detailed | Limited |
| Ease of completion | Takes more time, more difficult | Easy |
| Difficulty of designing question | Easy | More difficult to phrase to eliminate ambiguity |
| Ease of coding response | Difficult, more chance of error, maybe misinterpretation | Easy |
| Likelihood of unexpected response | Probable | Unlikely |

**Examples of different types of response**

*Likert Scale*
5 = strongly agree, 4 = agree, 3 = uncertain (or neither agree nor disagree), 2 = disagree, 1 = strongly disagree.

*Visual analogue scale*
Respondents are asked to mark a cross on a line which best describes how they feel:
Very satisfied.............................................Not at all satisfied
1     2     3     4     5     6     7     8     9     10

*A delighted/unhappy faces scale*[2]

☺ ☺ ☹

## Pilot phase

Trying out your draft questionnaire on people who will not be in your final survey should detect problems with your questions or method of distributing and collecting the questionnaires. You should never miss out this pilot phase because you are short of time. Even if you are using

▼

**Have you experienced any difficulties in phoning into the surgery to make an appointment?**

a validated questionnaire that is well tried and tested it is still worth piloting your method of distribution and collection.

The number of people you choose for your pilot will depend on the number in your study population and how straightforward your method is. If you have a complicated study design and need to encompass minority groups, then your survey method will need to include sufficient responses from each of the particular subgroups of the population and the numbers of people you recruit for your pilot will be far more than for a simple study of easily accessible subjects. If you read published studies in the journals you can see that pilots often involve 10–50 people depending on the circumstances.

### Benefits of a postal questionnaire survey

- ▶ It is relatively cheap as it does not involve interviewers.
- ▶ One skilled person can design the project, whilst less skilled staff undertake the data collection.
- ▶ Repeatable.
- ▶ Can be distributed over a wide geographical area.
- ▶ A snapshot of views.
- ▶ Can obtain the views of many people, although the bigger the survey, the more costly it is.
- ▶ There is no observer bias, as there may be with interviews.

### Drawbacks of a postal questionnaire survey

- ▶ Chasing up non-respondents by post or phone increases costs and effort.
- ▶ Obtaining results is relatively time consuming allowing for time taken to chase up non-respondents and carrying out analyses.
- ▶ Response rates tend to be lower than for interview surveys.
- ▶ People who are illiterate, have learning disabilities, are visually impaired, have poor concentration, suffer mental health problems, elderly people and those from ethnic minority groups whose first language is not English will be under-represented as they are unlikely to complete questionnaires.
- ▶ The researcher cannot be sure who has answered a postal questionnaire; it has to be assumed that the person to whom the questionnaire was addressed is the one who responds.
- ▶ It may be easier for respondents to give dishonest answers to a postal questionnaire than in a face-to-face situation.
- ▶ No opportunity for the respondent to clarify the question if they do not fully understand it.
- ▶ No opportunity for dialogue or participation in decision making.
- ▶ People may be asked to give their opinion about services they know nothing or little about (see boxed example of the NHS patients' survey).
- ▶ Complex data collection and interpretation require good organisation.
- ▶ No explanation as to why respondents think in a particular way.

> **The first national survey of NHS patients**
>
> This 20-page postal survey of the general public asked about their experiences of using the NHS and what they felt about the services provided. Recipients of the unsolicited questionnaire were asked to respond with their views even if they had not had any contact with the NHS recently. Questions asked respondents for their experiences of access to the GPs, nurses and practice services where they were registered, whether a GP of the same sex as the respondent was available at their practice, how good their relationships and communication with the GP were, out-of-hours care and hospital referrals.

## *A protocol for carrying out a patient survey using a self-completion questionnaire*

- ▸ Decide the exact question being posed.
- ▸ Write down the purpose of the survey.
- ▸ See if the information you intend to collect already exists elsewhere and if so, obtain those data and abandon your intended study.
- ▸ Define your target population.
- ▸ Consider the extent of resources available to undertake the survey: your and others' time, expertise in designing, coding and analysing, funds for printing and postage, etc.
- ▸ Write out the timetabled protocol: the number to be sampled (ask a statistician or other expert for help with deciding the optimal number needed), how sampling will be carried out, description of pilot phase, the method of delivery of the questionnaire (e.g. postal survey, newspaper survey, interview), how completed questionnaires will be returned, how and when non-respondents will be chased up, the outcomes by which achievement of the purpose will be measured, methods of dissemination, likely action plan resulting.
- ▸ Obtain ethical approval if appropriate (*see* Chapter 5).
- ▸ Identify if an established and valid questionnaire already exists. If so, find out if you can use it or must obtain permission from the author to do so.
- ▸ If no appropriate questionnaire exists, design your own. Carry out preliminary work gathering people's views as to the content and purpose of the survey. Keep going with your fieldwork until you feel that you have heard all the issues and are familiar with the language and phrasing the target population generally use.
- ▸ Frame your questions using the usual terminology favoured by your target population, making sure you will have elicited enough information in the questionnaire to be able to make decisions about how to progress afterwards.

▶ Set out your questionnaire to win the 'hearts and minds' of the respondents to encourage a good response rate; it must be attractively laid out, seem relevant and acceptable, as though it will provide useful information and be easily answered.

▶ Try to keep a written questionnaire reasonably short, for example two sides of A4, but don't achieve this by cramming in far too many questions in a small font size.

▶ Include a covering letter to explain the purpose of the questionnaire, what will happen to the results and how confidentiality will be maintained.

▶ Add the name of the author and return address on the questionnaire in case it gets separated from the covering letter.

▶ Do not include any unnecessary or meaningless questions: for instance, 'marital status' is included in many questionnaires and the results discarded because respondents find the question ambiguous, e.g. 'single' might mean 'unattached and available', 'attached but not married', 'divorced and not in long-term relationship'.

▶ Prepare the coding sheet for alternative responses.

▶ Try out the questionnaire on people who will not be amongst your sampled population. Ask them to tell you if they perceive any problems with the wording or the method or if any other questions should have been included and do not ask them just to answer the draft questionnaire. Check that the coding frame works for the responses you receive for both the open and closed questions. Refine your questionnaire and method accordingly.

▶ Number your target population and allocate each with a code number. If you write the code number in the top right-hand corner of the questionnaire form, then respondents may be invited to snip it off if they prefer, to ensure that their identity will not be known to anyone at all.

▶ Start your survey. Make it easy for respondents to return the questionnaires, with stamped addressed envelopes, a freepost address, easily accessible collection boxes, etc.

▶ Remind non-respondents once or twice, depending on your resources, time frame and how important it is to have as good a response rate as possible.

▶ Code the responses in the completed questionnaires; arrange for two people to independently code the open questions and compare how closely their interpretations of the themes and options agree, reaching a consensus where necessary.

▶ Enter the coded responses into a statistical software package such as Minitab or SPSS. The responses should be entered twice and any discrepancies between the two sets of results corrected. If you do not have access to a software package you can tot up the responses by hand but it will be more time consuming and you won't be able to do any statistical tests.

▶ Analyse the results. Look at the tallies summarising the numbers of respondents giving alternative answers to each question. Decide if you want to test whether there are any statistical associations between two answers; only do this if you can justify ordering the test and don't just trawl through all your data looking for any significant differences or correlations.

▶ Present your report with results that are easily understood by non-experts – perhaps as tables with percentages, bar charts, a graph or a pie chart. Include an honest assessment of the biases of the method and the limitations of the interpretation that might be put on the results. Add conclusions and an executive summary or abstract at the beginning that picks out the key points.

▶ Disseminate and share your results, change practice and systems as appropriate, feedback the results and any changes that are planned and have occurred to the respondents and patients and the public in general.

---

**The covering letter for a postal questionnaire survey should:**

▶ contain a brief description of what the purpose of the enquiry is, why the recipient has been selected, who is involved, what the time period is

▶ mention whether the respondent's reply will be anonymous or whether you are using a code number and if so, who knows to whom the code number refers

▶ emphasise confidentiality, stating that no individual or practice will be identified in any report, if this is so

▶ give a date by which you hope to receive a reply

▶ state how the completed questionnaire is to be returned, e.g. in a stamped addressed envelope

▶ thank the respondent for their help.

---

A rough time schedule for undertaking a questionnaire survey is about a year to 18 months by the time that the preparation, questionnaire design, piloting of the questionnaire, data collection and analysis and the writing and dissemination of the report are taken into account.

# Patient satisfaction surveys

You might wish to assess patients' satisfaction with your practice, the trust's way of working or the services available in a locality or a district. Doing patient satisfaction surveys became quite a popular pastime for the NHS in the early 1990s when medical audit was being developed. Patients tended to be asked for their views on their surroundings and how the NHS systems were working: what did they think of the waiting room, were they satisfied with the arrangements for making appointments or getting repeat prescriptions? Questions were usually relatively superficial and did not delve into complex areas.[3] Because the nature of the enquiry was so general, satisfaction rates were often high. The purpose of these patient satisfaction surveys was often to be seen to be taking part in the then-new audit culture, rather than to try to pinpoint problems and rectify them.

The new push to involve patients and the public in planning and delivering healthcare might have the same effect – of encouraging health professionals to be seen to be engaging in politically correct exercises but which may be relatively meaningless. Unless the organisers have a clear purpose and intent to make changes as a result of the information and co-operation they obtain from the public and others with whom they work feel part of the exercise and are willing to make appropriate changes too, they will not use the right tools or select the right methods. Nor will issues be probed at a deep enough level to give information about causes and problems to recommend changes that will make a difference in practice.

If you decide to compose your own questionnaire for a patient satisfaction survey, you should follow all the good advice on the content and protocol described above.[4] But it will probably be simpler and more valid to use a tried and tested questionnaire instead. The use of some questionnaires is restricted by copyright and requires a fee for photocopying them and surveying study populations. Some questionnaires can be purchased from commercial outlets with manuals that give details of scoring and comparable results.[5]

Before you start, you will have to decide what level of satisfaction will be acceptable to you. The specific level will depend on the circumstances of your enquiry and how important it is that people should be satisfied. It may not be possible to please everyone; the satisfaction threshold in a situation where you are asking a cross-section of the population about the allocation of resources that affects them directly, so that there will be some winners and losers, will differ from that in a consultation with the same population about a service that benefits them all.[6] Some feel that an 85% patient satisfaction level should be the threshold below which the organiser should be concerned about the level of dissatisfaction, whilst others accept a 70% overall satisfaction threshold.

You should already have ideas of alternative approaches you might take as a result of a patient satisfaction survey, so that you can follow through with a plan of action. People will only co-operate in future surveys if they see changes resulting from previous ones and don't perceive the next survey as just another public relations exercise.

> **A community mental health trust acts after a patient satisfaction survey indicates a lack of privacy**
>
> The Stafford-based trust runs patient satisfaction surveys as a regular part of its work. The surveys are just one component of a range of activities that encourage users and the general public to be involved in the delivery of mental healthcare. They work to a minimum threshold of 70% overall patient satisfaction.
>
> A recent survey of inpatients identified privacy as a problem for some patients. The ward beds were rearranged to provide more privacy and plastic hoods were fitted to telephones sited in the corridor to allow for private conversations. Poor communication between some patients and the nurses and doctors looking after them also emerged as a theme of dissatisfaction. The care plan system was reviewed and changed as a result.

# Newspaper surveys

Another method of administering a survey to the general public is via a free local newspaper. This has the advantage of being quick to distribute to many in the population. But you will have little control over exactly what is printed or who receives the questionnaire; it might be people passing through your locality and the newspaper may not be delivered to all the households you thought were covered. Nevertheless, useful information can be obtained in this way, as is illustrated in the example given.

## *Benefits of a newspaper survey*

- ▶ Cheap administration, so long as the newspaper editor makes no charge for inserting it.
- ▶ Gains publicity for the issue as well as undertaking the enquiry.
- ▶ Quick method – no chasing up of non-respondents.
- ▶ Strengthens contacts with local press, paving the way for future articles on the same health topic when results are available, or other stories.

## *Drawbacks of a newspaper survey*

- ▶ Low response rate.
- ▶ No control over who responds – some people may reply more than once if they pick up several copies of the newspaper, especially if there is a free prize draw to tempt them.

▶ Respondents are unlikely to be a representative section of the population.

▶ Newspaper staff may misprint questions or omit whole or parts of questions to fit within their space constraints.

▶ Non-English speakers unable to answer questions, although this may be partly minimised by advertising an option in minority languages for people to ring in for translated copies.

▶ Similar difficulties for poor readers, elderly people, etc. as for the drawbacks of a postal questionnaire survey, described previously.

---

**A newspaper survey to elicit the general population's views about what the authorities might do to improve health in the city of Stoke-on-Trent[7]**

A questionnaire was composed to test out the population's views about what the city might do to improve the health of the local community, based on previous findings from various community development projects in the district. The questionnaire was printed in a free newspaper delivered to 110 000 homes and businesses and left at public access points. Prizes were offered to the first six entries drawn out of a hat after the closing date. Five hundred and twelve completed questionnaires were returned. Analysis showed that the age groups and gender mix of respondents were reasonably similar to those of the local general population. Around a fifth of respondents described themselves as being of Asian, Bangladeshi or Pakistani origin, compared to 3% of the local population being of ethnic minority origins, according to standard statistics. Respondents were more likely to be non-smokers compared to the known figures for the adult population, indicating a tendency to be more health conscious than average.

The most frequently given views, by at least three-fifths of respondents, of how the city might tackle poor health in the community were: 'targeting misuse of drugs', 'reducing air pollution', 'promoting good diet or nutrition', 'providing an antismoking campaign' and 'targeting alcohol abuse'. The most frequently cited factors that at least two-fifths of respondents thought made them less healthy were: 'too much stress or worry', 'lack of exercise', 'poor diet', 'very low income', 'fear of violence or crime' and 'animals fouling in the street'. These results are informing the development plans of the partners who commissioned the survey – the health authority, local authority, chamber of commerce, the community trust, the university and voluntary organisations.

Some of the main drawbacks to the survey were: the low response rate (which meant that the respondents were not representative of the general population, although the age/gender mix was similar); the printed questionnaire in the newspaper had many mistakes and

*continued*

*continued*

omissions; not knowing whether people who completed the questionnaire fulfilled the study criteria and were adults living or working in
the city (some people who responded lived 100 miles away, having
picked up the questionnaire at the local railway station; some gave
their age as being under 18 years); and a disproportionately high
percentage of people responded in an ethnic minority language
because the person who translated the questionnaire into other
languages hand delivered questionnaires to them and urged recipients
to respond.

# Interviewing

Interviews may be administered in person or over the telephone.
An unstructured interview is an informal conversation initiated by
the interviewer in which the person being interviewed describes their
experiences and views. A structured interview is one where the interviewer works through a standardised questionnaire asking the questions
in the same order and in the same way to each subject. A semistructured interview is also based upon a questionnaire but has a freer
format in that the questions are taken in the order that follows the flow
of the conversation. The interviewer usually sums up at the end of the
interview, to check that the interviewee has had an opportunity to
express their views, and invites any additional comments.

A protocol for undertaking a study where the information is
obtained by interview is similar to that given for a postal survey above
in that the same good practice in question construction should apply.
The interview schedule should be piloted and revised accordingly. The
analysis should be thought through when phrasing the questions, to
make sure that the coding of questions for later analysis is relatively
easy. The aim of the interview and context of the survey should be fully
explained to the interviewee. Written consent should be obtained if
appropriate, depending on the purpose of the study, the sensitivity and
intrusiveness of the questions and characteristics of the person being
interviewed.

The questions making up the interview schedule should start with
straightforward, easily answered ones that put the interviewee at ease.
The skilled interviewer asks the questions in an unbiased, non-threatening
way and encourages confidences. Good interviewing skills include listening attentively, probing as appropriate, reflecting back what was said,
noting and responding to non-verbal cues, showing empathy and being
flexible about the depth and range of the questions, depending on how
the interview is progressing. Biases arise when the interviewee is too

eager to please the interviewer or alternatively takes a dislike to him or her. The interview should ideally be held in a room which is quiet, private and on neutral territory but many interviews take place in less than ideal conditions such as in a public place, for instance a street. Many interviews are audiotaped and transcribed to allow at least one independent person to listen to the tapes later and make a separate report of the themes and detailed responses that can be compared with the main researcher's version to reduce the chances of bias and mis-interpretation of the interview material.

---

**An interview survey to determine the general public's views about NHS prescription checks intended to detect and deter fraud**

Face-to-face interviews were undertaken with a representative sample of 2047 adults in England, Wales and Scotland in one week of 1998. The object of the survey was to assess the acceptability of a change in practice whereby people collecting prescriptions from the pharmacy or surgery where they were dispensed would be asked in future to provide evidence of being exempt from paying for prescriptions, if they were claiming this was so. Two-thirds of the general public were 'very much in favour' and a further fifth were 'slightly in favour' of the checks on entitlement to free prescriptions. Virtually everyone was in favour of the government's plans to tackle all types of fraud within the NHS, with less than 2% being against. The survey included open questions that invited people to say in their own words why they were in favour of the checks. The results helped to decide the content and message of the public information campaign and if there had been resistance to the change of policy then more information would have been given to explain and justify the reasons for the checks.

---

The interviewer should be careful to label the cassettes of the interview with the interviewees' names, the date, time, etc. It is useful to add their own comments and insights in brackets to the transcript of the tape, whilst they can recall them vividly, and highlight important phrases in the text – these might be new or surprising information, summarising points or phrases that are characteristic of the speaker. The interviewer may refine the interview schedules in the light of earlier interviews to focus down on particular areas or extend the enquiry if unexpected material has cropped up.

> **Gaining the carer's perspective[6]**
>
> Two hundred and seven carers were interviewed using semistructured questionnaires, about three months after the people for whom they had cared had died of cancer at home.
>
> Three-quarters of carers had not been told of support available from local charities and half had not been given advice on financial help. A minority had had difficulty getting professional help. Domestic help was often needed earlier than it had been arranged. Overall, three-quarters of the carers considered that the professional support they had received was 'excellent'.

## Benefits of interviewing

- ▶ Better response rate than postal survey.
- ▶ Explores issues in depth.
- ▶ Interviewee more likely to trust interviewer and confide in him/her than to divulge sensitive information in a paper exercise.
- ▶ Can record non-verbal cues as well as spoken answers.
- ▶ Flexible questioning allows the interviewer to follow up interesting leads, especially if an unstructured interview schedule is used.
- ▶ Questions can be clarified if they seem ambiguous or unclear and if the interviewee has a poor grasp of the language, poor concentration or limited intelligence.
- ▶ You can be sure that the person responding is the person you are interviewing in a face-to-face situation.
- ▶ The interviewee is more likely to give an answer to every item on the interview schedule than if he or she were completing a postal enquiry.

## Drawbacks of interviewing

- ▶ The social and ethnic characteristics of the interviewer may affect the responses.
- ▶ The interviewer may bias the responses if the interviewee is aware of the interviewer's own views.
- ▶ Relatively expensive in skilled interviewer time, travelling time, planning and piloting the interview schedule, transcribing and analysing audio tapes (may take a secretary up to eight hours to transcribe a one-hour tape).
- ▶ Analysing data requires interpretation of themes and content and therefore two researchers are needed to work in parallel to compare and agree findings.
- ▶ Interviewees may give the responses that they think the interviewer wants to hear, rather than honest answers.

▶ If people are being surveyed whose first language is not English, it is cheaper for an interpreter to translate a written questionnaire for a postal survey than for bilingual interpreters to attend interviews.

### Telephone interviewing

This is a cheaper option than face-to-face interviewing, as travelling time is saved. Unless the interview is short, the interviewer may have to phone first to make an appointment to conduct the telephone interview at a more convenient time. It may be better to send a covering letter explaining the purpose of the exercise and what is involved, similar to the covering letter accompanying postal questionnaires, described before.

▼

**You cannot be 100% sure who you are interviewing on the phone.**

Some researchers have found that telephone interviewing produces 'socially more desirable' responses than is the case with a postal questionnaire method about the same topic.

Just as for a postal survey, the interviewer cannot be 100% sure who is answering the questions on the other end of the phone. Only people with telephones can respond and this restricts the socioeconomic mix of the population included in your survey. The telephone is a good way of including people living in different geographical areas or targeting specific groups of the population.

You might use a computer-assisted telephone interview (CATI) technique to help gather the data.[8] This is a computer program set up with alternative pathways of responses where the interviewer is prompted by computer-generated questions. As the respondent gives an answer this triggers the next appropriate question in the sequence. If you do use CATI, the interview schedule will have to be well structured and the pathways of responses will need to be fast and operator friendly. Using CATI makes coding much easier as it is done automatically and the data analysis is very quick, so that the time taken to undertake a survey is minimised. It is a relatively cheap way of completing a large number of interviews and appears to be an acceptable method of collecting information from the public. Market research companies often use this method.

## References

1   Dolan P, Cookson R and Ferguson B (1999) Effect of discussion and deliberation on the public's views of priority setting in health care: focus group study. *BMJ*. **318**: 916–19.

2   Bamford C and Jacoby A (1992) Development of patient satisfaction questionnaires: I. methodological issues. *Quality in Health Care*. **1**: 153–7.

3   Avis M (1997) Incorporating patients' voices in the audit process. *Quality in Health Care*. **6**: 86–91.

4   Grogan S, Conner M, Willits D and Norman P (1995) Development of a questionnaire to measure patients' satisfaction with general practitioners' services. *Br J Gen Pract*. **45**: 525–9.

5   NFER-Nelson (1999) Clinical psychology assessments and training catalogue. NFER-Nelson, Windsor.

6   Jones RVH, Hansford J and Fiske J (1993) Death from cancer at home: the carers' perspective. *BMJ*. **306**: 249–51.

7   Chambers R, Jacobs B and Schrijver E (1999) *Stoke-on-Trent City Population Survey*. School of Health, Staffordshire University, Stafford.

8   Harris D, Grimshaw J, Lemon J *et al.* (1993) The use of a computer-assisted telephone interview technique in a general practice research study. *Fam Pract*. **10**(4): 454–8.

# CHAPTER 4

# Working in groups, gauging public opinion, gaining consensus

This chapter will describe how to use a variety of qualitative methods to gather information and views from patients, carers and the general public. The methods covered are:

► focus groups: discussion groups
► special interest patient groups: user groups, carer groups, patient participation groups, disease support groups
► general public opinion: opinion polls, citizens' juries, standing panels, public meetings, neighbourhood forums
► community development: local community development projects, healthy living centre activities
► consensus events or activities: Delphi surveys, nominal groups, consensus development conferences
► informal feedback from patients: inhouse systems such as suggestion boxes, complaints.

## Focus groups[1,2]

Focus groups offer a controlled method of enquiry into specific topics. They typically last between one and two hours. Groups are usually made up of between seven and ten people, but their size can range from four to 12 members. You need a minimum number of people to contribute ideas and a maximum number for interaction and to give everyone an opportunity to be involved. A moderator leads the group through a series of pre-prepared questions and themes, keeping the discussion constructive and focused on the topic in hand. If there is an observer, he or she remains outside the discussion but is available to advise the moderator how the discussion is progressing through the planned agenda. The discussions are often audiotaped so that comments made by the participants can be referred to and cited in any report. The person convening the focus group, the moderator, and the observer should have prepared well for the meeting and have captured the major issues as themes of five or six questions to be posed to participants. The questions should be framed to trigger discussion about feelings and attitudes as much as knowledge or experience.

The focus group should be held in a comfortable private room. The venue should be fixed on neutral territory if there is any question of a conflict of interests in relation to the issues to be discussed. Minimise external noise or any other intrusion that might distract the participants and disrupt the discussion.

Focus groups are composed of people who are similar to each other or share a common characteristic, such as having the same health problem, e.g. asthma, or the same experiences, e.g. recently discharged from hospital, or being in the same socioeconomic group. The topic, themes for discussion and participants themselves should all be selected as being the most suitable to fulfil the purpose of the focus group. It is best if the participants are complete strangers. Otherwise, they may feel unable to be entirely honest about what they think in front of people they know or will be working with. If some or all know each other, the moderator will have to take account of this.

The group moderator should be skilled at establishing a non-threatening and supportive atmosphere for the participants. Everyone should feel that their contributions are valued. They should feel reassured by the moderator being non-judgemental and setting out the questions in a neutral tone.

Rewards for participating vary: perhaps refreshments afterwards or a gift voucher for a nominal amount or as much as £30 for attending,[3] with travelling expenses reimbursed.

The purpose and goals of the focus group should be clearly set out. The aim is to identify issues that had not previously been thought of, gain new insights about the issues from the participants' perspectives, gauge the strength of feeling about different issues and spot emerging trends. Focus groups help the organiser to learn the vocabulary of users which they can use later in a report or when describing the services for the public, to seem more in tune with or have more appeal to a particular user group, for example young people. The group is not expected to reach consensus or agree a plan of action or make recommendations. The organiser should continue to convene more focus groups to consider the same questions until no new information emerges. This might be by using the same questions with similarly composed groups or with groups that have a different mix of participants from a variety of backgrounds. Many people run three or four focus groups before feeling that they are not gathering new information but the exact number depends on the variability within the discussions and numbers of contrasting views expressed. The views of focus groups are not necessarily representative of the wider community, much depending on who was recruited to participate in the groups and how they were selected.

> **Focus groups identify the patient's view of the management of breast cancer in Sandwell**
>
> Twenty women who had been treated for breast cancer were randomly selected from the hospital patient administration system and invited to two parallel focus groups. The purpose of the focus groups was to hear about the women's experiences of treatment for breast cancer at Sandwell Hospital, in order to use that information to improve the service for future patients. All the women had undergone treatment at least 18 months before and were all physically well as far as hospital records showed. Discussions were audiotaped and transcribed. A clinical psychologist acted as facilitator and a nurse as observer. Eight aspects of treatment for breast cancer constituted the agenda for discussion, which was developed by three clinical staff (the facilitator, a surgeon and breast care nurse), the Chief Officer of the then Community Health Council and two staff specialising in clinical effectiveness.
>
> A main theme of discussion for both groups was the importance of good information being given to patients throughout the care process: breaking the bad news about the diagnosis being cancer, knowing about the range of sources of information, having opportunities for discussion about surgery and its implications prior to surgery, making information and counselling available for patients' families and before providing after-surgery treatment such as chemotherapy. The draft copy of the report was approved by the participating patients before the final report was distributed to staff. Findings were fed back to the clinicians for them to recommend changes to the service.

## Benefits of a focus group

- Gains insights into perceptions and feelings and the framework of understanding of the issues in question.
- Explores participants' attitudes, language and priorities.
- Information is gained over a short time frame.
- Needs only one skilled person – the group moderator.
- Relatively low cost – resources required for planning and preparation time, venue and hospitality for several short group meetings, compiling report.
- Can be used at different stages of healthcare: before (needs assessment), during and after a service is conceived and established.
- Stimulates debate.
- May include people who cannot read or write.
- Particularly good at identifying cultural values.

▶ People can participate who would usually say they have 'nothing to contribute' as they are more confident about joining in discussion as one of a group than as an individual.

▶ Can elicit views about 'embarrassing' topics.

▶ Participants can express criticism where they might not do so with another survey method.

▶ Good as second-line method to back up the results from a quantitative survey or to look at one of the findings in depth.

### Drawbacks of a focus group

▶ Narrow purpose – focusing on perceptions rather than recommendations or action plan means that further follow-up work is required.

▶ Not necessarily representative of a cross-section of opinion or the population.

▶ Participants are not necessarily 'informed' about the issues being discussed and they might change their views if they were given more information and the opportunity for deliberation.

▶ Marginalised groups are unlikely to participate.

▶ Difficult to use when subjects are geographically dispersed.

▶ Costs can be higher than expected when the transcription costs of the discussions are taken into account.

## Paying for consumer participation

Unlike research, where participants are not usually paid, it is essential that patients and others acting as consumers who are actively involved as partners in health and social care consultations, be paid. If an

---

**Example of payments for consumers participating in public consultation activities**

A team from the Centre for Health Policy and Practice at Staffordshire University trained cohorts of young people, older people and people disabled by society to carry out public participation on a range of topics of interest to them. The consumers were paid either £4 per hour plus travel /other expenses, or £5 per hour to include expenses (they chose which). The consumers were paid for undertaking ten 3-hour training sessions and for carrying out research/participation, analysing data and for their time involved in writing up and disseminating the findings.

employer pays health professionals, managers or researchers for attending meetings or carrying out such work, then consumers should be paid too. There are no hard and fast rules about how much to pay consumers for their involvement, but the *Guide to Paying Consumers Actively Involved in Research*[4] sets out guidance on expenses as well as time, expertise and examples of rates. This is available on the web at www.conres.co.uk/pdf/guide_to_paying_consumers110302.pdf.

## Budgeting for consumer involvement

It is essential that you budget properly for consumer involvement.

---

**Checklist for budgeting for consumer involvement**[4]

✔ Cost of recruitment, e.g. adverts, seminars.
✔ Extra time to facilitate recruitment and training of consumers.
✔ Cost of training researchers, health professionals or managers to work with consumers.
✔ Travel expenses for consumers.
✔ Out of pocket expenses for consumers.
✔ Childcare costs for consumers.
✔ Carer costs for consumers, e.g. someone to accompany them or look after dependants.
✔ Support worker costs for consumers.
✔ Translation or interpreting costs to facilitate the involvement of hard to reach groups, e.g. Linkworker.
✔ Data analysis support.
✔ Hire of rooms or equipment to facilitate access/participation for those with disabilities.
✔ Dissemination costs, e.g. conference, publication, advertising.

---

## Job description

If you think about the consumer role as you would any other role in the NHS, then it is obvious that you will need to develop a job description. This will make it clear to consumers what is expected of them and the terms and conditions of their involvement. In addition, it will help you to define exactly what skills, experience, knowledge and abilities you feel that consumers would need to have to play an active role in the research and participation initiatives. A draft job description is outlined in *Involving Consumers in Research &Development in the NHS: Briefing notes for researchers*[5] which is available on the web at: http://www.conres.co.uk/pdf/involving_consumers_in_research.pdf.

---

**Checklist for a job description**[5]

✔ Skills, experience, knowledge and abilities they need currently.

✔ Skills and abilities they will need to develop.

✔ What is expected of consumers.

✔ Ability to work alone, or as part of a team.

✔ Ability to travel, if required.

✔ Extent of commitment that is required, e.g. time, activities.

✔ How much consumers will be paid, e.g. how much they will be paid for their time, whether they will be paid for travel or more for different tasks, whether carers, or carers for dependants will be paid.

✔ What elements consumers will be paid for, e.g. travel time or just the time spent participating.

✔ How consumers will be paid, e.g. cash, cheque, food tokens or other vouchers.

✔ When consumers will be paid, e.g. will they be paid at meetings or at a later date? Specify how long they will wait. Do not expect consumers to wait too long for expenses. Can you can provide financial advances?

✔ Specify whether they will need to use their own equipment, e.g. their telephone and when and how costs for this will be reimbursed.

Add information about what evidence of expenditure is required such as receipts for taxi or bus fares; and the potential impact on benefits, allowances and tax.

---

*Impact on state benefits, allowances, National Insurance, tax and charities*

Paying consumers can have an impact on their benefits and one of the barriers to user participation may be they feel that payments will affect their benefits. Although it is the responsibility of the person receiving the benefit to notify the Benefits Office of any additional income, it is important that you advise consumers about this issue and that you can refer consumers to people who can advise them such as the Job Centre

Plus, the Citizens Advice Bureau (CAB) or the Department of Work and Pensions (DWP). Receiving money may also have an impact on National Insurance and tax – the Inland Revenue can advise on this.

---

**Information about benefits in relation to public participation programme**

The Wolverhampton Health Action Zone's *Steps to Employment Programme* aimed to help mental health service consumers to access training that would eventually lead to employment. However, many potential clients did not become involved, as they were afraid that this would affect their benefits. The Programme overcame this barrier by inviting Job Centre Plus to attend a meeting to explain to the group what they could and could not do in order to keep their incapacity benefits. This included therapeutic earnings and the hours that they could attend further education.

---

## Involving patients through user, support, participation or voluntary groups

There are at least five types of patient or voluntary groups: support groups, campaigning groups, social and/or healthcare providers, advice or information-giving organisations, Patients' Forums, Patient Advice and Liaison Services (PALS) and Independent Complaint Advisory Services (ICAS). Few areas log all their existing voluntary organisations or map the different kinds of services they provide. In North Staffordshire there are more than 450 voluntary groups and probably others which are not known to the authorities. Some are stand-alone local groups and others branches of national organisations. Consequently, there is a great deal of duplication by different groups. Many people who might benefit from their help are not aware that the services exist.

*User* or *support groups* might be able to:

▶ raise general and specific concerns about treatment
▶ point out where complaints systems and services are not user friendly
▶ ask for more information about drugs and their side effects
▶ meet with the authorities or managers to tell them what standards and services they want
▶ help to train NHS staff so that they understand users and their needs better.

They generally offer support to people suffering a particular disease condition, such as Parkinson's disease, or who have a general problem, such as mental ill health, although a users' forum for mental health may not encompass all conditions such as dementia or age groups such as young or elderly people. Carers may also be welcomed and supported at user groups.

---

**Users involved in training health and social care professionals**

Mental health service users from MIND have been involved in training social services staff at Uttoxeter. To avoid overworking keen service users, the use of video-recorded user input is being discussed.

---

The *Expert Patient Programme* is a national movement to set up self-management training programmes for patients with chronic diseases, and it has been rapidly adopted by trusts across the NHS in England.[6] The belief behind the approach is that 'Patients can only be fully involved in their treatment if they have the requisite knowledge and skills. And if the health professionals who treat them recognise those skills and knowledge, working in partnership to devise and implement individual pathways of care.'[6] The expectation is that by gaining self-management skills such as problem solving and goal setting, participating patients will become more confident in managing their own conditions and contributing positively in their treatment and care. Evidence for the effectiveness of the expert patient programme includes: reduced severity of symptoms, significant decrease in pain, improved life control and activity and improved resourcefulness and life satisfaction.

*Campaigning groups* or *pressure groups* may be a mixture of people with personal or caring experience of the problem or disease or well-intentioned people from the community. Their activities include fund-raising, promoting the cause and highlighting their key concerns through public awareness raising using the media, the press and any other appropriate medium, via schools and better literature.

*Social and healthcare provision* by the voluntary sector is of a far greater quantity and quality than many of those working in the NHS are aware. Health professionals are often surprised to find that voluntary groups provide healthcare from paid and qualified staff. Health authorities and local authorities commission health and social care services from voluntary organisations.

*Advice-giving* help by voluntary organisations is underutilised by doctors and nurses because of their lack of awareness and understanding of the services provided by voluntary groups. One example where the distance between general practice and the voluntary sector has led to patients not being made aware of potential benefits is illustrated in the box opposite.

**Primary care professionals do not make patients aware of the advice that is available from Citizens Advice Bureaux (CABs) with the result that some patients miss out on potential benefits**

When CAB advice and support sessions have been piloted in general practices, substantial unclaimed benefits have been raised for patients on low incomes who have had no previous contact with the CAB services.[7] Some work has shown that clients visiting CAB services sited in general practices are more likely to be older and have a disability or long-term illness than those visiting traditional high-street CAB services. The take-up of CAB sessions located in primary care settings in pilot projects appears to be dependent on primary care team members' attitudes to working with external organisations and their extent of awareness, confidence and knowledge of what constitutes an appropriate referral for CAB advice. A way forward lies in finding methods of increasing the understanding of primary care staff and those working in CABs and other voluntary organisations of each others' roles and capabilities in enhancing patients' health and well-being.

*Patient participation groups* may be a mix between user or support groups, campaigning and advice groups, providers of social care and fundraisers. Members of patient participation groups may be invited or self-selected. The objectives of different groups include: involving patients in planning services; co-ordinating volunteer programmes (for example, volunteer-run transport schemes for the elderly, visiting the practice or hospitals); developing health promotion and illness prevention; providing feedback on existing services; and fundraising. Some general practices have used patient participation groups to inform decisions about services or the delivery of primary medical service (PMS) pilots.

Patient participation groups flourish in some trusts and general practices but relatively few practices have such groups: there were thought to be about 160 UK practices with patient participation groups in 1996.[8] They are most likely to be successful when the objectives of the group are clear and there is continuous support from the practice or trust. The boxed example overleaf illustrates the 'clients' council', a form of patient participation group in one community trust.

**A clients' council established at a community mental health trust in Stafford**

The council was set up in 1997 to involve and empower users of the trust's services, by gathering users' views and prioritising their issues. It has a core of ten lay members who form the steering group and meets bimonthly with equal numbers of representatives of the trust – nurses, ward managers and trust management – to try and solve individual and group concerns. All of the council's representatives are either service users, former service users or carers. Most of the service users are outpatients. The council's open meetings give other users opportunities to express concerns or ask questions about anything to do with mental health issues or the trust, without any member of staff being present. Meetings are held in community premises and rotated around the locality. The trust is encouraging the council to become increasingly autonomous by establishing an executive core within the steering group to meet and liaise with members of the trust's executive team several times a year.

The Royal College of General Practitioners endorses the philosophy of patient participation groups and user involvement in general through its Patients' Liaison Group – *see* box.

**The Royal College of General Practitioners' Patients' Liaison Group**

The Group exists at the College to:

► communicate areas of patient concern
► consider ways of achieving a consistent and equitable quality of care for all
► encourage the involvement of patients in their own care and in the development of the health service at all levels
► foster relations between patients and their medical advisers on the basis of openness, equity, honesty and individual integrity
► encourage College faculties to involve patients in all aspects of their activities. (*Terms of Reference*, 1999)

The membership of 12 has a majority of lay people. The Chairman of the Patients' Liaison Group has a seat on the College's council as an observer, but no voting rights. Their main concerns are that patients are involved in planning and delivering NHS care at all levels,

*continued*

> *continued*
>
> in training healthcare staff, setting standards in clinical governance, helping with staff selection and training and contributing to guidelines about best practice and quality. They want to see the NHS take the public on board in a meaningful way in a culture of openness and accountability. Then, patients can expect to receive information about morbidity rates, be regularly updated about their progress, share information about the costs of treatment and doctors should not feel threatened by patients asking questions about their care or risks of treatment.

# Gaining the general public's opinion

Involving the local community in making decisions about local health services should mean that services are better targeted at what the population wants and needs and public support for the services provided is promoted.

> **2001 census targets health**
>
> The 2001 census sent to 32 million households contained three general questions on health in order to target local needs and inform the allocation of resources. The questions asked respondents how they considered their health had been during the past 12 months, whether they were an unpaid carer and whether they suffered from a long-term illness.

## Public consultation

Health and local authorities do hold public meetings if a major change to local service provision is being planned, such as closing a local hospital. But some public meetings are really public relations exercises, where decisions that have already been made behind the scenes are paraded as still being up for discussion. The issues raised in public consultation are often not explicit enough and may centre on establishing people's preferences, dissociated from the hard choices that would have to be made if new services were to be set up in line with their stated preferences. Sometimes the disinvestments that will be needed are discussed but as they are theoretical, they seem to be remote or apply to another section of the population from those being consulted.

There may still be a public outcry about losing established services, even though this is a logical stage in switching resources to support the public's priorities.

*Thank you for coming to our public consultation..... to hear what we've decided to do.*

▼

**Public consultation.**

**Shaping services for older people in North Staffordshire by an extensive consultation with the local community[9]**

The consultation exercise has actively involved more than 1000 local people. The local trusts, the health authority and two neighbouring social services departments were all lead partners in formulating the proposed development plan following widespread consultation through:

▶ a series of local 'stakeholder' conferences providing opportunities for service users, carers, voluntary agencies, private and statutory service providers and commissioners to participate in developing the proposals by a two-way exchange of views and ideas

*continued*

*continued*

▶ meetings with a wide range of groups of older people with special needs including: people with visual or hearing problems, Asian males and females, an Afro-Caribbean group, people with learning disabilities, people from a Polish community

▶ local professionals including: GPs, a League of Friends, local councillors, non-executive members of the health authority and trusts, staff groups

▶ a questionnaire survey inviting comments on the report of the stakeholder conferences preceded by several meetings of around 300 older people organised by Age Concern and statutory agencies (435 questionnaires returned out of 2000)

▶ public briefings: a stand in a local shopping centre; press release

▶ correspondence with local MPs.

Some changes were piloted whilst the consultation continued as the proposed development plan was circulated widely for comments and views over a further three-month period. Older people were recruited as 'ambassadors' to discuss the plan with various groups and report their comments. A further series of meetings was planned to review and debate the proposed plan with all those who contributed during the first phase of the consultation. Additional efforts were made to consult individual older people and their carers who did not belong to groups, using a 'carers' bus' as a way of contacting very isolated people.

**'What You Said' – the responses to the 'Our City – Our Health' city-wide consultation in Sheffield[10]**

Around 5000 people responded to this consultation exercise: 1421 were individuals, 90 interagency groups or organisations, 11 professional groups and 92 community groups. The aim of the consultation was to find out what people thought were the main health issues and problems affecting their health and to look for ideas about what could be done to improve health in Sheffield. The consultation methods included using facilitators to talk to people, groups and agencies, holding discussion groups, producing audio and written materials to inform the debate, appending a questionnaire to discussion documents. The responses were mainly written but included phone calls, memos, audio and videotaped comments and suggestions. The largest single issue was concern about the environment, with many people making links between their health and the environment in which they lived. Poverty and discrimination were both frequently mentioned as having major effects on people's ability to enjoy good health and well-being.

On the whole, consultation exercises fail to reach most of the population. On the other hand, some public opinion exercises are intentionally targeted at people or organisations who are already informed about the issues in question – see the illustration in the box below of the Human Fertilisation and Embryology Association's (HFEA's) public consultation on how banning payments to egg and sperm donors should be implemented.

---

**Responses to the national public consultation on the implementation of withdrawal of payments to egg and sperm donors**

The consultation paper was sent out to fertility centres and special interest groups across the UK; patients, the general public, clinic employees, health professionals and campaigners were all invited to respond. The consultation document contained background information about the topic and a mix of open and closed questions. The purpose of the exercise was to consult on how the HFEA's policy to end payments to donors might be implemented. The responses received were not expected to necessarily dictate the HFEA's future actions; they welcomed the information but reserved their right to take a different course of action if the majority of public opinion was not in line with their established policy on the matter.

In the event, 176 completed questionnaires were returned, of which 154 were from individuals and 22 were corporate replies from organisations, groups or centres. Responses were mixed and ranged from whole-hearted support for the HFEA's policy to accusations that the policy to end payments was out of touch with the real world and the numbers of donors would be drastically reduced as a result. Strong feelings spilled over outside the consultation to be expressed in the national press, too. The question behind the consultation about how to implement the policy was widened by respondents into challenges to the actual policy itself and included many other related issues such as preserving the anonymity of donors, access to treatment, the ethics and practical considerations of egg sharing as a method of donation and the importing/exporting of sperm to and from the UK.

As a result of the consultation and the HFEA's further reflections on the issue, the policy was softened and payments to donors of egg and sperm gametes were retained until acceptable alternatives were identified and introduced.

---

The National Institute for Clinical Excellence (NICE) has recently set up a Citizens' Council to provide advice relating to social, ethical or moral questions which arise in the Institute's work. Members of the Council are representative of the general population and explicitly exclude people working in the NHS or private medicine or in healthcare industries, patient groups or those who lobby on their behalf.

The Council used deliberative techniques derived from experience with citizens' juries (see page 54) at its first meeting where members concluded what features of diseases and conditions and features of the patient should influence decisions about clinical need.[11]

One cynic recently said: 'Money spent on public consultation is worthwhile if the public are behind you because you can make the changes happen quicker. If the public are against you, that just delays things for a while whilst you find another way or try again a year or two later'.

## Open meetings of strategic health authorities and trusts

The public is entitled to attend strategic health authority and trust board meetings. Few of the public usually attend, although there is often a representative from the local press present.

The government is committed to opening up NHS board meetings to the public. 'Public board meetings should not be orchestrated events with decisions taken behind the scenes in a closed session.'[12] NHS boards should publicise their meetings well in advance and arrange their meetings so that the public feel they are welcome to attend and copies of the agenda and meeting papers should be available. Closed sessions should be limited to those areas of board business where real harm to individuals might result, such as discussion about staff disciplinary matters.

## Opinion polls

*Ordinary* opinion polls, such as those operated by market researchers in the street, do not give the public a chance to form a considered opinion. Results given off the cuff may be misleading, as some people would change their minds and beliefs if they were better informed, as the boxed example shows.[3]

---

**Effect of discussion and deliberation on the views of focus group participants[3]**

Sixty patients from two urban general practices in North Yorkshire each attended two focus group meetings, two weeks apart. The participants' views about setting priorities in healthcare were systematically different at the end of their second focus group meeting compared to the beginning of the first meeting, after they had been given opportunities to discuss the issues and had time for personal reflection. About half of the participants initially wanted to give a lower priority to smokers, heavy drinkers and illicit drug users receiving healthcare but by the end of the second meeting, about one-third of these no longer wanted to discriminate against such people.

*Deliberative* opinion polls demonstrate that many members of the public will change their minds about an issue when given information and a chance to deliberate with experts and others from different social backgrounds. They measure the informed opinion of typically 250–600 randomly selected members of the public on a particular issue. The participants who are recruited reflect the profile of the wider population to which the issue applies. They are well briefed before the event which usually lasts 2–4 days. Participants deliberate on the issues in small groups and frame further questions to ask experts and politicians in full plenary sessions. The participants do not attempt to reach a shared view. Actual opinions and changes in opinion are measured over the polling event.

Other ways to inform the public include using standing citizens' panels and convening citizens' juries.

## Standing panels

Typically a 500–3000 sample of the local population comprises a standing panel. As the participants remain on the panel, their opinions can be tracked over time. A sample of the population is usually recruited as panel members by post, telephone or hand-delivered letter. A proportion of the panel will be regularly replaced. The panel may be consulted as a whole by questionnaire or in sections through focus groups or workshops. Bradford and Lewisham are two areas with several years' experience of standing panels. Trusts may be able to use a local standing panel set up by others, as with the one illustrated in the box below in Stoke-on-Trent. Some areas have established several 'health panels' with around 12 members of the general public on each, who meet several times a year with the health authority to discuss health topics. Somerset,[13] Croydon and Lambeth, Southwark and Lewisham health authorities have set up a series of health panels.

---

**A standing panel is set up in Stoke-on-Trent**

Four thousand citizens were selected at random from the electoral register and invited by questionnaire to take part in the consultation exercises and help guide the city council's future work. The final panel has 650 volunteers who provide a representative cross-section of age, geographical and social mix from all parts of the city.

The panel's first consultation exercise was to revise and review the city's corporate plan by identifying people's concerns, needs and aspirations. Seventy percent of the panel responded. The panel members were most concerned about: increasing community safety

*continued*

*continued*

and encouraging crime prevention; facilitating and encouraging the economic development of the city; raising educational achievement and opportunities for all people of all ages in the city; developing and enhancing opportunities to meet the social and health needs of the people. In addition, the panel urged that local action be taken to target the misuse of drugs; this was added to the corporate plan, having not previously featured as a priority in the city council's plan.

Standing panels.

## Citizens' juries[14]

Citizens' juries have been developed in the USA and Germany to give those in authority information about ordinary citizens' opinions. A typical jury has 10–20 people. The group meets to give a considered view on a set task, framed as a question. Jurors discuss and debate the issue in the light of written and verbal evidence from witnesses and experts before producing a report. The jurors look at the often complex issues from the point of view of a group of citizens rather than as consumers, experts or members of a special interest group. An independent facilitator is on hand to help the process. Citizens' juries have been used by local authorities to inform decision making and more recently, they have been tried in a health context.

Reports from areas in the UK that have experimented with citizens' juries have found that it was important to take time to decide the question to be put to the jury and express it in words that were seen as meaningful and appropriate to lay people.[14] Typically, jurors are asked to choose between options drawn up by the health authority or to develop criteria to guide decisions on a particular issue. Each of these citizens' juries[14] had a steering group who shaped the question, prepared the information and evidence for the jurors, identified witnesses, involved the 'stakeholders' who were likely to be the ones to take any recommendations forward and a wide range of others with a broad platform of interests. In each case a project worker took 5–6 months to set up, organise and run the citizens' jury. Jurors were not elected by the local population but were recruited by independent organisations such as market research companies. They were selected to reflect the profile of the local population with respect to age, gender, employment status, ethnicity and geographical spread. Some organisers realised retrospectively that it would have been better if jurors had not known one another prior to the jury being convened.

The organisers learnt that it was best if witnesses limited the giving of their evidence to 15 minutes followed by 30–45 minutes for questions from the jury. A brief written summary of the information they presented was helpful to the jurors. A typical jury lasted four and a half days and jurors were paid £200 plus expenses. Most limited the numbers of observers to 12 and placed them behind the jurors so that they were less distracting. The most important feature of the venues where the juries were held was that the jurors, observers and witnesses could remain separate at refreshment breaks. The jury report was typically written by the project officer employed by the jury sponsors who were members of the steering group and not the health authority. The jurors approved the reports before they were submitted to the commissioning body – the health authority or local authority. The reports were practical and included recommendations for future policy and practice.

▼

**Citizens' juries.**

The outcomes of the citizens' juries piloted in the UK have varied from instances where the jury's report has influenced local decision making to examples where the jury's verdict coincided with other people's earlier recommendations which then took on a higher priority.[14] The commissioning body should make the jury's report public and either plan to follow the jurors' recommendations or justify why they do not do so.

The evaluation of citizens' juries found that '… the cost of running a jury … was a lot more expensive in terms of both staff time and cash needed than the usual methods employed to involve the public …'.[14] The costs were estimated to be between £16 000 plus staff time[14] and £30 000.[15]

Some of the citizens' juries tried in the UK have been one part of a greater public involvement exercise, whilst others were a one-off event.

**A citizens' jury hears evidence about access to health information**[16]

Eighteen local people in East London heard evidence about residents' access to health information, from medical educators, health information experts and GPs amongst others. The jury advocated setting up health information points in public places, where people could get advice about medical conditions, where to get appropriate care, benefits and housing. The jury also recommended that health professionals were kept up to date about new information sources and that the NHS complaints procedures be better co-ordinated.

**A citizens' jury debates who should make decisions about rationing**[17]

Portsea Island Primary Care Organisation in Hampshire commissioned a citizens' jury of 14 members to give an independent verdict about who should take responsibility for rationing medical treatment. The jury heard evidence from GPs, health authority officials and MPs over a two-day period. The jury recognised that GPs could face a conflict of interest between financial and clinical issues but concluded that GPs were best placed to make decisions about rationing so long as primary care groups consult widely and are open and accountable to the public.

**Benefits of citizens' juries**

> ► May influence local decision making.
> ► Demonstrate the commissioning authority's accountability to the public.
> ► Keep the commissioning authority and experts in touch with the 'real world'.

**Drawbacks of citizens' juries**

> ► Time consuming to set up and run.
> ► Expensive.
> ► Involve relatively few people.
> ► Commissioning authority may disregard the jury's verdict.

# Community development

Community development is targeted at people who tend to be excluded from society or who share a common characteristic. That might be that they live in the same locality or have a common feature in their lives, such as being a young single parent or living on the same housing estate. Community development aims to help people 'tackle for themselves the problems which they face and identify to be important and … empower them to change things by developing their own skills, knowledge and experience and by working in partnership with other groups and with statutory agencies'.[18] It involves interaction between communities and statutory and other agencies, using consultation and advocacy. Those undertaking community development use methods like focus groups and observation to inform the developmental work and to evaluate whether it has been effective.

Trained community development workers bring local people together to:

▶ 'identify and support existing community networks, thus improving health

▶ identify health needs, in particular those of marginalised groups and those suffering inequality

▶ work with other relevant agencies, including community groups, to tackle identified needs

▶ encourage dialogue with commissioners to develop more accessible and appropriate services'.[19]

In particular, community workers may gather evidence about successful models used elsewhere and get interested parties to work together with the local community to see how such models might be adopted and funded locally.

All these activities are at the heart of primary care trusts' responsibilities. Few of the previous primary care commissioning groups took on community development or public involvement and so trusts will benefit from working with established community development workers now to make best use of their skills. Champions of community development feel that the techniques could help trusts to 'develop decision-making processes that truly involve users'.[19]

---

**Evolving a healthy living centre from community development work**[20]

Health and social needs of the deprived community of Chell have been undertaken through several community projects over two years that have assessed the population's 'needs' from an NHS perspective and the community's 'wants' by listening to local people as groups

*continued*

*continued*

and as individuals. As a result, a healthy living centre is being created and will offer a gymnasium, a drop-in café, youth facilities, some community education sessions and multipurpose rooms for various community activities, community health services and medical services provided by a local general practitioner with a nurse partner.

The business case for the healthy living centre recognises that 'the local community needs to have a say as to how the centre develops in future'. The overall justification for the centre is: 'to promote collaborative work with the local community, to improve access to information and advice which can help local people take more control of their own situations and to encourage activities which empower and raise the aspirations of the local community'. The centre will involve the local community in its management structure and 'take full account of its views'.

## Community participation in primary care groups and the health action zone in Tyne and Wear[21]

GPs and others in Newcastle and North Tyneside have been working with community involvement initiatives since 1994. The Newcastle Health Partnership has a strategy for city-wide community participation that aims to help local communities act on their own health agendas. Special efforts have been made to include black and ethnic minorities, gay and lesbian groups, older people, adolescents and people with a physical or sensory disability. The community development worker in the west end of Newcastle is accountable to the local community rather than the health authority.

Health priorities emerged from the 90 local groups involved in the initiative and were taken up by health services management. The community worker and two lay members of the health action group have places on the local primary care trust's board. An annual local health conference is attended by more than 200 local people and develops priorities for the year's proposed health commissioning. Their experience is that public involvement leads to a greater understanding of local health issues and new ways of tackling them. The two-way dialogue improves relationships and gives the public an insight into the pressures on health services.

## Health parliaments

Potentially, a parliament might consist of up to 120 members from statutory and non-statutory organisations and members of the public. The aim is to provide a democratic decision-making process to discuss, debate and decide upon a way forward for local strategies and developments.

---

**A youth parliament**

One health action zone that plans to put public opinion at the heart of all its activities is setting up a 'youth parliament'.[22] They hope to use the parliament to test whether they are making a real difference to health on the ground. The organisers have chosen this approach in response to the frequent calls from young people consulted during other local community studies that they want to 'feel they have a voice and are listened to'.

---

Different varieties of methods have been tried for involving young people.

► Youth councils, such as in Devon, where 20 members aged between 14 and 25 years are elected by affiliated organisations which include schools and youth clubs. The council is supported and advised by several council departments and the local education department. The aim of a youth council is to participate in decision making. Members may meet regularly or come together as a one-off event.
► Young people's forums, such as in Manchester, where the members represent more than 20 youth groups. They advise staff from the health authority and city council on the delivery of services to young people.
► Young people's networks, such as in Cardiff where 1000 young people are involved and have advised the Welsh Office about the contents of the Patient's Charter for young people.

## Rapid appraisal[23,24]

The research team gathers information from as many different sources as possible about the needs of a local population. This will include reviewing documents held by different agencies and directorates of the health authority, local authority, city council, chamber of commerce, voluntary groups, the education sector, and other reports from various community development projects, local general practices and official statistics. The researcher interviews a small number of key informants, who represent local people, professionals, different organisations and agencies. Focus groups and postal surveys may also be employed. The local press may help by advertising the presence of the project, attracting information, publishing the results and inviting comments.

### Benefits of rapid appraisal

- A multidisciplinary team of investigators reduces bias from the researching perspective.
- It is community orientated.
- The different sources of information give many dimensions to the problems and a more complete picture than if the exercise had fewer facets to it.
- Interviewing local people and professionals ensures that the results are current.
- The approach combines three perspectives: of individuals (the interviewing phase); population wide (the reports, interviewing); and community groups (interviewing, reports).
- The technique results in a plan of action for the prioritised problems and does not just stop at the information-gathering stage of other public involvement exercises.
- Those involved in carrying out and participating in the appraisal are likely to own the results and be committed to co-operating with the action plans.
- The technique encourages closer collaboration between health and social care organisations, housing, education and the public.
- Encourages local networking.
- Enables the local community to be involved in decision making.

---

**Listening to local voices: adapting rapid appraisal to assess health and social needs in general practice in Edinburgh**[23]

The technique of rapid appraisal was used to build a profile of a community living on a council estate of 670 homes. The three sources of information used were: existing documents about the neighbourhood; interviews with a range of informants; and direct observations. The interviews and focus groups identified six priorities for change, many of which were not directly health related:

- arrange for a bus to come into the estate
- create multiple small areas and dog-free zones
- run advice-giving and educational activities in the community room
- improve the running of local general practices

*continued*

*continued*

► ask the local pharmacist to be more helpful about collecting and delivering prescriptions
► provide residents with practical advice about dealing with their difficult physical environment.

The rapid appraisal initiative took 12 meetings of the development team and 45 interviews; in retrospect, the team thought that the first 25 interviews with ten residents and 15 local workers would have been sufficient. The investigating team comprised a general practitioner from one of the two general practices serving the estate, a health visitor, the local community education worker and two local social workers, backed by a part-time secretary. The team members allotted about four hours per week to gathering the information over the project time period of three months, conducting the interviews in pairs. Two focus groups discussed and prioritised the problems identified and explored potential interventions.

The local newspaper reported the study in detail and invited comments on the findings and proposals. The team concluded that 'an expanded primary care team can use rapid appraisal as a first step in identifying and meeting local health needs. It facilitates a multidisciplinary approach and complements quantitative methods of assessing need'.

## Drawbacks of rapid appraisal

► Biases may occur if the majority of informants selected share similar views and people covering the full range of opinions are not included.
► Bias from interviewers/researchers occurs if they are unskilled or their own views, ethnicity and gender influence the interviewees unduly (see 'Drawbacks of interviewing', p. 33).
► The appraisal is carried out over a short time frame.
► Written documents and reports used as sources of information may be out of date (e.g. the national census).
► Reports of previous work may refer to communities by ward, whilst the appraisal may be of part-communities that cross wards.
► The project work is time consuming, especially if local health professionals are involved and undertake the appraisal alongside their usual professional duties.
► Much organisation is required to arrange the interviews, especially with those from hard-to-reach groups who may be more difficult to tie down or persuade to join in.
► There are opportunity costs for all those taking part in the information-giving and gathering sides of the exercise.

*In-house feedback from patients*

The practice or trust could encourage public and patients to use feedback boxes more than they are used at present by making them more obvious and publicising changes that have resulted from such feedback. As with other methods of public or patient involvement, the usefulness of the exercise depends on the extent to which the practice or trust enters into the spirit of the exercise and uses the information obtained. If every positive or adverse comment is scrupulously logged in a record book by whoever receives or overhears it, then a more complete picture is built up, rather than an occasional note of praise or complaint being received. A culture should be encouraged where it is accepted as being in everyone's interests that patients feel able to air problems and difficulties before they become significant complaints.

One of the components of clinical governance that should be high-lighted as an important aspect not to be overlooked is for the NHS to 'celebrate' its success. Collecting positive suggestions and feedback is one way of achieving such a positive approach.

---

**General practices involve patients in feedback exercises to design their Patient Charter**

One of the successes of Staffordshire Medical Audit Advisory Group's Patient Charter project was to encourage general practices to design their own charter with a set of 'rights' and 'responsibilities' that were realistic for that practice. Of the 55 practices replying to a follow-up questionnaire in 1997, 38 (69%) had involved patients in setting or commenting on the standards, in various ways.

---

According to a recent report, general practitioners are 13 times more likely to be sued than ten years ago.[25] The general public are said to be more conscious of their rights and more likely to sue. The informal complaints procedures in practices and trusts do defuse many com-plaints at an in-house stage rather than involving the health authority, NHS ombudsman or General Medical Council. Any complaints pro-cedure should be well publicised, speedy, open, impartial and focused on resolving grievances and improving services.

Lay feedback has proved valuable for assessing standards of GPs' care as part of the Royal College of General Practitioners' quality award system. A lay assessor is part of the 'Fellowship by Assessment' visiting team, for instance.

# Consensus exercises

Nominal groups, consensus conferences and the Delphi technique are three different types of consensus exercises. Consensus methods may be used to help make decisions where there is an overload of information about a subject and some of it is contradictory, so that it is unclear what is the best way forward. The experts involved contribute wide-ranging information, some of which may not be published and would not be available except by talking to the experts. Their insights into the problem or issue being considered are as important as the knowledge they contribute.

## *Nominal group*[26–28]

The nominal group is a structured group method used for generating ideas in answer to a specific question. The group meeting usually lasts about 1–2 hours and involves 5–9 people, although as many as 12 might participate. The structure tends to encourage everyone's participation and reduce any disproportionate input from the more dominant personalities in the group, so that the ideas and plans arising from group discussion are more democratically determined. The facilitator should be experienced in group work rather than be an expert on the topic under question. The purpose of the group meeting should be clear and the question or problem explicitly stated so that all participants are sure about the task they are addressing.

▶ *Stage 1*: Each participant silently generates ideas in writing for 5–10 minutes in response to the question posed, jotting down ideas as brief phrases.
▶ *Stage 2*: Each participant takes it in turns to read out one idea at a time in a 'round robin'. The participant should contribute their best ideas first. These are listed verbatim on a flipchart by the facilitator or another group member and as sheets are filled they are hung up on available furniture and walls with Blu-tack. Participants can link new contributions into others' earlier ideas.
▶ *Stage 3*: Each idea is clarified if necessary and discussed. Duplicate ideas are combined. The separate ideas are numbered.
▶ *Stage 4*: The participants vote for their most important priorities from the numbered ideas using a pre-agreed voting system. In one example, participants allocated five votes to the item that they felt was the most important, down to one vote for the item that was the fifth most important for them.[28]
▶ *Stage 5*: The group discuss their action plan and priorities in the light of the voting and reach a consensus about how they will address the original question.

**Benefits of a nominal group**

- ▶ The method generates many ideas.
- ▶ The technique is useful for identifying problems, exploring solutions and establishing priorities.
- ▶ It encourages everyone to contribute and avoids a few people dominating the group.
- ▶ Participants are equal members of the group.
- ▶ It is a way of involving the 'grassroots' in the decision-making process.
- ▶ Participants may be of mixed backgrounds, for example from different disciplines or a mix of NHS staff and patients.
- ▶ The written generation of ideas encourages the commitment of the participants in taking part in the planned action.
- ▶ Only one skilled facilitator is needed.
- ▶ The technique produces an answer with few resources.
- ▶ Decisions are taken at the close of the meeting.

**Drawbacks of a nominal group**

- ▶ People have to be able to read and write.
- ▶ Group members have to make themselves available at the same time for the hour required, which may be difficult in tight work schedules.
- ▶ The ideas may be ill informed or impractical.
- ▶ For the nominal group to have a positive outcome, those in authority have either to accept the group's solution or participate themselves to be part of the process.
- ▶ The nominal group would have to be combined with other techniques for a complex issue or one that significantly affected others outside the sphere of influence of the group.

## *Consensus development conference*[27,29]

Consensus development conferences have been used in industry on such subjects as air pollution and plant technology. Consensus is reached by a panel of 10–20 lay people who have been well briefed prior to the event. The panel sits at the conference where members develop further understanding of the scientific or technical issues, 'in dialogue' with experts on the subject. The conference is open to the public who may also put questions to the experts. The panel members retire to try to reach a consensus view and then agree the contents of an independent report. The co-ordinator of the consensus development conference should be a skilled group leader and a disinterested party as far as the topic of the conference goes.

The NHS has used consensus development conferences as a means by which health professionals can reach a verdict about best practice in particular health conditions. In two examples, 21 medical experts came together for one day to agree a consensus statement on the diagnosis and recognition of depression and 17 medical experts (most of whom were the same as on the first occasion) considered the management of depression in the same way, on a second occasion.[30] Specific questions were addressed by a presenter with a prepared paper followed by another speaker giving their viewpoint on the first presentation. An agreed consensus was then reached after extensive general discussion. The draft consensus statement was circulated to participants for further refinement and approval. The consensus was owned by the participants themselves, rather than the Royal College of Psychiatrists and Royal College of General Practitioners whom they represented. The consensus statements were published as guidelines for other health professionals. These consensus conferences were run in much the same way as those which considered air pollution and plant technology, except that a wider audience was not present and prior briefing meetings were not held as the participants were already experts in their fields.

### Benefits of a consensus development conference

- ▶ A one-off event means an answer is available in a short space of time.
- ▶ Specific consensus statements can shape and catalyse action plans.
- ▶ Those in authority may be invited to officially review consensus statements as a way of involving those in power, such as managers, to take forward the agreed consensus view.
- ▶ The consensus conference publicly highlights the issue in question.

### Drawbacks of a consensus development conference

- ▶ The validity of the consensus reached is dependent on the credibility of panel members.
- ▶ There is an assumption that the participants can produce sound decisions.
- ▶ The stricter the criteria set to indicate the minimum level of agreement at which consensus may be taken to have been reached, the harder it is to obtain consensus.
- ▶ Large-scale consensus studies need political and professional support if they are to be actioned.
- ▶ The validity and reliability of consensus statements have not been established.[29]

## Delphi technique[27,31]

Relevant individuals are recruited, usually on the basis of their knowledge and willingness to contribute. They may be experts in the field or ordinary citizens depending on the purpose and topic of the exercise. Many Delphi studies used in the NHS in the past have involved experts or informed advocates, rather than a random sample of participants, but the technique can be applied in many different circumstances and using experts is not essential.[31] The Delphi technique is a postal exercise consisting of three or four rounds (usually) of a self-completed questionnaire, the results from each being summarised and fed back to the participants after each round so that they may confirm or amend their previous responses at the next round. The Delphi process ends when the participants stick by their previous opinions and do not wish to make changes or too few participants continue to return completed questionnaires.

▶ *Stage 1*: Potential participants are asked whether they are willing to take part in the exercise. The amount of work, numbers of rounds of the survey and time commitment are explained. They should be asked to make a definite commitment to participating throughout all the rounds of the survey as the validity and reliability of the survey will hinge on retaining as many respondents as possible at every stage of the process.

▶ *Stage 2*: Participants contribute their opinions about the topic or issues that are being considered; these should be their own views, expressed freely, and then posted back to the organiser. The opinions of all the participants are summarised and grouped together. The questionnaire (version 1) for Stage 2 is built up from these opinions into statements to be considered by the participants in the next round.

▶ *Stage 3*: Participants rank their agreement to each statement in the questionnaire (version 1). This may be a simple 'yes/no' type of response or a more sensitive answer that portrays the degree of agreement or certainty with which the participant is responding to the statement. The rankings are summarised and included in the next version of the questionnaire (version 2). The organiser should encourage as good a response rate as possible and this might be by allowing three weeks for the participants to respond with a further reminder to non-respondents, for every round. Freepost envelopes and clear instructions will make responding easier and more likely.

▶ *Stage 4*: The next questionnaire (version 2) is circulated and participants rank the refined statements in the light of the given summaries of the group's range of responses. At this stage they are being asked in essence to confirm or amend their answers to the previous questionnaire (version 1).

▶ *Stage 5*: Responses are again summarised and ranked. If consensus has been reached, the survey may cease, but it is more usual to repeat the process one more time (Stage 6) to see if any more respondents wish to amend their views.

▶ *Stage 7*: The final results are fed back to the participants.

### Benefits of a Delphi survey

- ▶ Anonymity of participants.
- ▶ The democratic process is designed to produce a representative opinion.
- ▶ Avoids dominance of one or more participants – everyone has an equal say.
- ▶ Low cost as experts contribute through postal means and time spent is minimal.
- ▶ Enables experts from a widespread geographical area to contribute.
- ▶ Captures experts' insights and knowledge.
- ▶ Individual participants can see where their thinking lies with reference to the range of opinions of the group.
- ▶ Individuals can change their opinion when they have had time to reflect.
- ▶ Judgement can be expressed as a summary of alternative responses rather than as a consensus statement.
- ▶ Can be used to explore policy issues or facilitate decision making.
- ▶ Larger numbers of participants give progressively more reliable outputs.

### Drawbacks of a Delphi survey

- ▶ Successive rounds occur over several months and participants' initial enthusiasm may wear off and they may not respond after two rounds.
- ▶ The importance of good questionnaire design is sometimes forgotten in the organisation of the series of communications with participants and speed of construction of the questionnaire to maintain the participants' interest.
- ▶ Anonymity may lead to a lack of accountability.
- ▶ It should not be used as the single method on which to base decisions, because it is an abstract method with participants reaching consensus away from the real world.
- ▶ Co-ordinating large groups of respondents can be time consuming and problematic (e.g. chasing up non-respondents, maintaining contact details).
- ▶ There is no opportunity for personal contact between participants for them to discuss or challenge views if they should wish to do so.
- ▶ Minority views or disagreements may be ignored in the summarising and reaching consensus processes and the holders of these views may become disenchanted by the survey if they feel that their views were discarded. They may consequently be more likely to drop out of successive rounds, so that there appears to be more convergence of opinion than is really the case.
- ▶ A paper exercise misses out the non-written communication of participants' views – tone of voice, body language, etc.

# Informal feedback from patients

Simple measures often work as well if not better than more complex systems, and cost little. Even if you have not had much success in the past with suggestion boxes or books for patients, re-consider using them. Patients say that they would welcome the opportunity to contribute suggestions and comments if they thought that someone would pay attention to them, and they knew how to go about it. So make sure that you fulfil both these points when inviting patient feedback.

One of the automobile assistance companies distributes a comment slip to every client to whom they are called out to help. Travel companies do the same on their client's return flights. You might not want to offer every patient the opportunity to comment routinely, but a targeted enquiry occasionally may give you valuable insights into the aspects of services and care patients value most, or would like to see improved.

Some practices have systems for recording every informal comment from patients rather than confine collection of patient feedback to formal complaints or extreme remarks. Reviewing this information every so often at a practice or trust meeting can shape developments.

▼

**Informal feedback.**

## References

1 Krueger RA (1988) *Focus Groups: a practical guide for applied research.* Sage Publications, California.

2 Kitzinger J (1995) Introducing focus groups. *BMJ.* **311**: 299–302.

3 Dolan P, Cookson R and Ferguson B (1999) Effect of discussion and deliberation on the public's views of priority setting in health care: focus group study. *BMJ.* **318**: 916–19.

4 Consumers in NHS Research Support Unit (CONRES) (2002) *A Guide to Paying Consumers Actively Involved in Research: for researchers and research commissioners.* CONRES, Winchester.

5 Consumers in NHS Research Support Unit (CONRES) (2002) *Involving Consumers in Research and Development in the NHS: briefing notes for researchers.* CONRES, Winchester.

6 Department of Health (2001) *The Expert Patient – A New Approach to Disease Management.* Department of Health, London.

7 Paris JAG and Player D (1993) Citizens' advice in general practice. *BMJ.* **306**: 1518–20.

8 Popay J and Williams G (eds) (1994) *Researching the People's Health.* Routledge, London.

9 North Staffordshire Health Authority (1999) *Better Services, Better Futures. Consultation Report: a plan for improving health and social care services for older people in North Staffordshire.* North Staffordshire Health Authority, Stoke-on-Trent.

10 Healthy Sheffield Partnership (1997) *What You Said.* Healthy Sheffield Support Team, Town Hall Chambers, 1 Barker's Pool, Sheffield S1 1EN.

11 Coulter A (2003) Citizen involvement in priority-setting. *Health Expectations* **6**(1): 1–2.

12 NHS Executive (1998) *Opening Up NHS Board Meetings to the Public.* Health Service Circular 1998/207. Department of Health, Wetherby.

13 Bowie C, Richardson A and Sykes W (1995) Consulting the public about health service priorities. *BMJ.* **311**: 1155–8.

14 McIver S (1998) *Healthy Debate? An Independent Evaluation of Citizens' Juries in Health Settings.* King's Fund, London.

15 Coote A (1999) Citizens' jury: a forum for health debate (editorial). *Update.* **18 March**: 485.

16 Safir J (1999) Citizens' jury in bid to educate public on health. *Doctor.* **1 April**: 8.

17 Woods C (1999) Citizens' jury commissioned by PCG: news in brief. *Health Service J.* **1 April**: 4.

18 Barr A, Hashagen S and Purcell R (1996) *Monitoring and Evaluation of Community Development.* The Scottish Development Centre, Voluntary Activity Unit, Department of Health and Social Services, Northern Ireland.

19   Fisher B, Neve H and Heritage Z (1999) Community development, user involvement, and primary health care. *BMJ*. **318**: 749–50.

20   Green A (1999) *Partnership Commitment to Redevelopment of Fegg Hayes Family Centre*. North Staffordshire Health Authority, Stoke-on-Trent.

21   Crowley P and Freake D (1999) Reaping the rewards. PCG partners, the public. *Doctor*. **8 April**: 62–3.

22   North Staffordshire Health Authority (1999) *Releasing Our Potential. Health Action Zone Implementation Plan*. North Staffordshire Health Authority, Stoke-on-Trent.

23   Murray SA, Tapson J, Turnbull L *et al.* (1994) Listening to local voices: adapting rapid appraisal to assess health and social needs in general practice. *BMJ*. **308**: 698–700.

24   Murray SA (1999) Experiences with 'rapid appraisal' in primary care: involving the public in assessing health needs, orientating staff, and educating medical students. *BMJ*. **318**: 440–4.

25   Pallot P (1999) Trust me, I'm a lawyer and I think we should sue. *Times*. **27 March**: B11.

26   Delbecq AL, Van de Ven AH and Gustafson DH (1975) *Group Techniques for Programme Planning: a guide to nominal group and Delphi processes*. Scott Foresman, Glenview, Illinois.

27   Jones J and Hunter D (1995) Consensus methods for medical and health services research. *BMJ*. **311**: 376–80.

28   Gallagher M (1993) Generating ideas for audit: nominal group technique. *Managing Audit Gen Pract*. **Winter**: 20–1.

29   Fink A, Kosecoff J, Chassin M and Brook RH (1984) Consensus methods: characteristics and guidelines for use. *Am J Public Health*. **74**(9): 979–83.

30   Paykel ES and Priest RG (1992) Recognition and management of depression in general practice: consensus statement. *BMJ*. **305**: 1198-202.

31   Linstone HA and Turoff M (eds) (1975) *The Delphi Method*. Addison-Wesley, Reading, Massachusetts.

# CHAPTER 5

# Doing it right:
# boring but necessary

Before you go on to apply your choice of methods of involving patients or engaging the public, it is important to make sure that you know something about the good practice and skills required to achieve meaningful results.

You should choose a method to sample your intended population that will include as representative a sample of people as possible. This requires a similar scientific framework as is necessary for any area of health research. The protocol for the study should be determined before any data gathering is carried out and include specific aims, appropriate methods and declared outcomes against which you can later evaluate the exercise. Any study should have adequate numbers or there will be unacceptable biases in the results. The extent of scientific rigour required for undertaking different episodes of consumer involvement will depend on the aims of the exercises, the degree of uncertainty which can be tolerated in the final conclusions and the likely variations of opinion in different subgroups of the population being engaged. The resources available – time, money, skills, staff – will influence the methods employed.

This chapter will consider:

► how to sample a population
► composing your sampling frame
► how to gain as representative a sample of the population for your exercise as possible
► patients' informed consent
► access to records
► best practice in planning, executing and writing up a survey or consultation exercise.

The actual construction of a questionnaire and carrying out of a survey was considered in Chapter 3. This chapter is concerned with making sure that you use a sound scientific approach to designing a quantitative survey or qualitative study.

# How to sample a population[1,2]

You don't have to ask the opinion of every patient registered with a general practice to obtain information about the availability of appointments to see the doctor or nurse. You can get that information by asking a sample of the practice population and looking at the appointments book. But to get an accurate answer, the sample you asked would have to represent the whole practice population. If you were to ask every patient attending a Monday morning surgery how easy it had been to make their appointments, you would be asking people who had been able to overcome any difficulties and succeed in getting appointments and who were able to attend the surgery during working hours. There might still be many people excluded from your enquiry who had not been able to get through on the phone or who had voiced their request in such a way that they had received a prescription or advice instead of an appointment or whose work prevented them from attending a morning surgery. And Monday morning surgeries might be of a different nature to those held on other weekdays when people had not had to store up their medical problems whilst the surgery was closed for two days.

## Composing your sampling frame

The *population* is the total group that you are interested in researching, for example mental health service consumers or people disabled by society. Unless the target population is very small (e.g. users with a very rare condition), or your resources infinite (which is very unlikely) you will have to select a sample of the population of consumers to work with.

In order to select a sample of the population, you will need to produce a *sampling frame*. A sampling frame is a list of population members from which the sample is drawn. This can be whatever you choose, for example all patients on a practice register, all patients admitted to a ward over a period of time, all mental health service consumers in one geographical area. However, you may not always have a sampling frame from which to select a sample. For example, you might not be able to identify a sampling frame for illegal drug users, or people caring for a relative with dementia.

As the following example demonstrates, getting the sampling frame wrong results in sampling error which can have disastrous consequences.

---

**Example of sampling error**

In 1936 a poll carried out by the Literary Digest predicted that Roosevelt would be defeated in the presidential election. Although it was based on a poll of several million people it was wrong. The reason for this was that the sample was mainly taken from car registration lists and telephone directories and in 1936 many voters did not own a car or a telephone and those who did would be much wealthier.

There are a whole range of *sampling strategies* that you can use and these are outlined in the box below. Your choice will vary depending on the research/participation initiative that you plan to carry out, the people you wish to include in your sample, whether or not you have a sampling frame and the resources available to you. The sampling strategy you choose can have an impact on the sample you end up with.

**Sampling strategies**

**Probability sampling**
▶ Simple random sampling – select a group of users/carers at random.
▶ Systematic sampling – select every *n*th user/carer from a list.
▶ Stratified sampling – sample within groups of the user/carer population.
▶ Cluster sampling – survey whole clusters of users/carers that you have sampled at random.

**Non-probability sampling**
▶ Convenience sampling – sample the most convenient group of users/carers you can find.
▶ Voluntary sampling – the sample is made up of users/carers who self-select.
▶ Quota sampling – convenience sample within user groups of the population.
▶ Purposive sampling – hand-picked sample of typical or interesting users/carers.
▶ Snowball sampling – building up a sample through users/carers who know people with similar conditions.

**Other kinds of sampling**
▶ Event sampling – using routine or special events as the basis for sampling.
▶ Time sampling – recognising that different parts of the day, week or year may be significant for certain users or user groups and sampling accordingly.

Modified from Blaxter L, Hughes C and Tight M.[3]

So the sampling technique you use is very important as you are trying to select a sample that can be trusted to represent the whole population to which the question underlying your survey applies. The stages in sampling a population are as follows.

*Identify the entire population connected with the purpose of the survey and the question you are asking*

The term 'population' is the entire group of people or things about which you want information; in the example given above, it is every person registered at one particular practice. If the investigation were about the treatment of asthmatics, the 'population' might be all people in one practice with asthma or all people known to have asthma or all people attending an asthma disease management clinic, depending on what the purpose of the survey was and the question posed. If the investigation was about the accuracy or completeness of record keeping, the 'population' could be the medical records of all patients in a particular practice or of the patients suffering from the disease in question or the paper or electronic versions of the records.

*Decide the important characteristics of your population that might influence your survey results*

A 'variable' is a characteristic of a unit of the population. You should identify important variables that might influence your results so that you can make sure that those characteristics feature in your sample to the same extent that they occur in the whole population from which the sample is taken. For instance, you might consider that age, ethnicity and gender are important variables in patients that influence how they respond to questions about lifestyle, travel or access to services.

*Think of ways to sample that are as little biased as possible*

Try to think of ways in which everybody in your population has an equal chance of being selected for your sample. A 'convenience' sample usually results in biases as it consists of a section of the study population that is easiest to reach. This might be the next 100 people to walk by. There may be good reasons why people with particular characteristics walk by where you are standing: if it is pub closing time you might find that many people who drink a good deal of alcohol are included in your sample or if it is the middle of the morning in a town centre you might find a disproportionate number of people who are unemployed or retired, compared to the demographic make-up of the local general population.

**Using a convenience sample**

A patients' discussion group was convened by an audit group to find out more about patients' experiences when they were referred from primary to secondary care, investigated, diagnosed and treated and discharged back to the community. One of the audit facilitators recruited a convenience sample of patients for the focus group by simply walking into four different outpatient departments and inviting one patient from each to attend the group. The four patients could bring a friend or relative for company. All four came and brought someone else too – a son, a wife, a husband and a friend. The focus group discussion went well. The chief executive and a hospital consultant from the trust and two local GPs were participants in the group too, which was facilitated by the audit team. Problems of communication were identified throughout their care pathways from when patients presented to the GP, to their visits to hospital outpatients, whilst inpatients in hospital and when they had been discharged home. Lessons were taken back to the GP practices and the trust and triggered a range of initiatives to improve communication to patients.

Volunteers are another source of likely bias. They often have a reason for contributing their opinion and might be delighted with a service or displeased with their treatment or more interested in a particular topic. Health-conscious people are known to be more likely to respond to health-related surveys. People who have strong negative views are more likely to take the trouble to respond to an opinion-poll type of survey than people whose views are 'middle of the road'. You need to be careful that people with personal agendas do not dominate a consultation exercise and limit proper public representation.

Random samples are less likely to be biased; that is, those in the sample population are more likely to be representative of the whole population if a fair method has been used in selecting them. It is best to decide on the actual number to sample in discussion with an expert such as a statistician or someone with considerable experience of surveys. You could number your whole population and then select every $n$th person or thing, where '$n$' is the whole population divided by the number you intend to sample. You could use random number tables to make your selection from a specialist book or an electronic package. Or you could pull numbers out of a 'hat' in the same way as tickets are drawn in a raffle, so long as every person or thing in your population has a number which is placed in that 'hat' and an equal chance of being selected. If you take a systematic sample by numbering every patient on a practice list, for example, and take every $n$th patient, you must be sure that the characteristics being studied are evenly distributed in the individuals of your population. You could not randomly select patients from a section of the alphabet because those with a disease or from minority cultures will be clustered with family names around certain letters of the alphabet.

---

**Random sampling patients from a practice register**

A GP practice in the West Midlands has set up a patient partici-pation group by inviting 16 people selected by random sampling from the age-sex register of its practice population. Seven patients accepted the invitation to meet and have since established a group. This method avoided the usual biases of a patient group formed from volunteers who are unlikely to be representative of the practice population and more likely to be champions of pet causes or the more vocal members of the community.

---

If you want to be in control of the way in which important charac-teristics or variables are distributed between the sample and the rest of the population, you might use *stratified sampling*. Sort your entire population out first according to whether they do or do not have the characteristics you have identified as possibly or probably having an important influence on your results. If this was gender, you will have two sections of your population – male and female. If an important variable was thought to be geographical location, you might categorise your population as to whether people lived or worked in an urban, rural or mix of urban and rural settings, or by the deprivation index for their locality. Then randomly select the sample in the same way as already described within each stratification or section of your popu-lation, weighting the number you draw from each category according to the frequency of that characteristic in the whole population or the proportions you want to study.

Bias is minimised by random sampling and by using a larger sample in proportion to the size of the whole population. The minimum number that you should include in your sample is worked out from a *power* calculation. Before you calculate the numbers for your sample, you need to decide how certain you wish to be that the results are correct (for the *confidence* in a statistical test) and how close you want the results to be to the true situation. The probability of detecting a difference when one actually exists is known as the *power* of a statistical test. Statistical significance can be misleading as differences which are inconsequential from a clinical or practical point of view (for instance, change of a few percentage points over time in satisfaction with a ser-vice) may be classed as 'significant' from a statistical test. Confidence levels of 95% are the norm for scientific tests. *Confidence intervals* give an idea of the range of uncertainty about whether a value in the results of a study lies within 95% (for instance) of the sample values from the whole population. The confidence interval gives you some idea of how close the results might be if you studied a large number of samples from the same population and how much the results from the sample in your survey can be trusted or how likely it is that your sample is truly representative of the whole population.

Most people use a statistician if they want to calculate the number of items or people they should sample that is likely to give them a statistical result from which they can be 95% confident that they have obtained a true result. Defining the right number to sample not only ensures that you have included enough people or things in your survey and won't need to repeat the exercise if the results are inconclusive, but also that you do not sample too many people or things, wasting your effort and intruding on an excessive number of people unnecessarily. There are 'ready reckoner' tables or formulae that you can use to calculate your own sample sizes.[4,5] One example given for medical audit of a population of 500 patients with a particular disease, such as hypertension, suggests that sampling 217 patients would be needed for 95% confidence that the results of the audit would be the same as if all 500 patients known to have hypertension were studied; whereas 176 of 500 patients should be sampled for a 90% confidence level and 278 of a population of 1000 for a 95% confidence level.[4]

If your sample size is likely to be too small because you have insufficient numbers of patients with a particular condition or characteristic, you could collaborate with other practices.

## Pilot your sampling method

Pilot your method on people or things which will not be part of your final study population. The pilot phase should check that the subjects find the questions used in the questionnaire appropriate and easy to answer and should also test the feasibility of your proposed method to see if the sampling system works and the resulting sample is likely to be representative of the population as a whole.

## Acknowledge the likely biases of your sample method

Sometimes it is not practicable to sample your population without significant bias. People's characteristics are not always known, your contact details may be incorrect or there may be a flaw in your method of sampling of which you were unaware until the results came in. You could find, for instance, that different ethnic groups vary in their willingness or ability to respond and that you have underestimated the barriers of language, culture or access to minority groups so that their response rates are low.

▼

**Consulting hard-to-reach groups is difficult and may be costly.**

**Ideas on sampling a minority group[5]**

Sampling minority populations and minimising biases are difficult.

▶ You might use census data to identify and work in geographical areas such as subdistricts or cities with a high proportion of people in the ethnic minority groups under study. But the ethnic minority population living in high-density areas may not be typical of that subgroup of the population in general. You may have to sample from several cities if you want to survey various ethnic groups as

*continued*

*continued*

> many cities have a preponderance of one ethnic grouping rather than substantial numbers from a range of different cultures.
> ► You could use a name recognition computer program to identify surnames likely to indicate people from an Asian community but surnames of other minority groups may not be so specific to a particular subgroup of the population as to render this worthwhile.

## Validity and reliability of a questionnaire[1,2]

Validity is the degree to which you are measuring what you are supposed to be measuring. Reliability is the degree to which you are consistently measuring what you want to measure.

You are more likely to gain valid and reliable results in a survey if you use a valid and reliable tool that has been developed and tested by others than one you have dreamt up yourself and not tested adequately. A lot of effort is wasted composing poorly designed questionnaires when a published 'off the peg' questionnaire would have provided a more valid instrument and obtained a more meaningful answer to the survey questions. The advantage of designing your own questionnaire is that you can collect exactly the information you want but if the information you collect is of doubtful validity and you would get a completely different answer if you repeated the survey on another occasion with the same questionnaire using different subjects, then the whole exercise is meaningless.

So before designing your own questionnaire, have a good search in the literature to see if you can find a questionnaire that has already been tried and tested. You can compare your results with the ones obtained in published studies to see if your population gives similar findings or if there have been changes over time. You cannot adulterate a published questionnaire and still expect it to be valid. Even relatively minor changes like removing items of choice from a list of options can destroy the proven validity of the original questionnaire. If you must add your own questions, do so at the end of an established questionnaire to have the least detrimental effect on its validity.

Two popular questionnaires, the General Practice Assessment Questionnaire[6] (GPAQ) (www.gpaq.info) and the Patient Enablement Instrument,[7] measure the quality of services that patients receive in general practice and patients' perceived ability to understand and cope with their illnesses and help themselves. The GPAQ measures access and availability, technical care, interpersonal care (including listening, explaining, time, caring and patience), continuity of care, trust, contextual knowledge (how well the doctor knows the patient), practice nursing care, referral and co-ordination of care outside the practice. The Patient Enablement Instrument focuses on how patients are coping with life or their illnesses and their approach to health. Beware of biases arising according to the mode of administration of the questionnaire or type of patients who complete the questionnaire in different circumstances.[8]

Another validated patient questionnaire is the Doctors' Interpersonal Skills Questionnaire (DISQ). DISQ is designed to give GPs structured patient feedback on their interpersonal skills within the consultation. It consists of 12 items that focus on the doctor's interpersonal skills, and includes aspects such as listening and explanation skills, warmth of greeting, respect for the patient, and ability to allow the patient to express their concerns or fears. Patients can suggest how the doctor could improve their service. It has been validated extensively and implemented in several countries including the UK, and with over 300 000 patients. It has been translated into six languages. You can find out more and view the DISQ questionnaire on http://latis.ex.ac.uk/cfep or email: cfep@dialstart.net.

## Ethical approval

GPs, nurses, therapists and other health professionals who are not connected to universities or working with academics do not always realise when they should seek ethical approval for research studies they conduct on their patients. If in doubt practitioners should consult their local research ethical committee when they are planning the study. The committee should be contactable through the strategic health authority which covers the geographical area in which the potential study will be based. The remit of the ethics committee includes:

▶ NHS patients, i.e. those subjects recruited by virtue of their past or present treatment by the NHS, including those treated under contract with the private sector.
▶ Fetal material and in vitro fertilisation involving NHS patients.
▶ The recently dead in NHS premises.
▶ Access to records of past and present NHS patients.
▶ The use of, or potential access to, NHS premises or facilities (including NHS staff).

You will also have to obtain permission to undertake the research from the NHS trust for which you work or that is hosting the research under its research governance framework.

## Obtaining and storing data

### The Data Protection Act (1984)

This requires that all personal data held on computers should be 'secure from loss or unauthorised disclosure'. Personal data are any information about someone else and include information collected in research or interviews about named subjects. The data held on computers in your workplace should all be registered with the Information Commissioner[9] but it is as well to check that the registration includes the types of details you propose to store. If you are working on the consultation or survey on your home computer, you should register in that capacity. The Registrar will need to know:

- your name and address
- a description of the data
- the purpose for which the data are being held
- sources from which data were/will be obtained
- people to whom data may be disclosed
- countries where data may be transferred
- the address where subjects can obtain access to the data about themselves.

## Statistical software

If you enter your data straight into a software package that has been developed for processing data from surveys then at the touch of a few keys, the computer will tally your results, produce bar charts, statistical tests, pie charts or graphs of your findings. You will see that researchers commonly cite an SPSS[10] software package in published surveys. You may be able to find out more about what particular statistical program might be available and appropriate for your study from your local university department or the information department at your trust or strategic health authority.

Entering data is best carried out twice over, especially if it is important that you do not make any mistakes keying in the data to your PC. Compare the tallies of both sets of results to see if there are any discrepancies between them and chase up and correct the reason for that. If the questionnaire has been set up for it, answers can be scanned straight into a computer. In that case scanning can read ticks and crosses placed in boxes, encircled numbers and hand-printed characters and digits.

## Informed consent

People should feel free to decline to participate in the consultation or survey without feeling that this will prejudice the quality of the care or attention they receive from you in future.[11,12] Consent is only meaningful if someone receives a full explanation of the intervention proposed. In the case of a consultation or survey, you should explain why you are carrying out the initiative and whether participating in the initial exercise could lead to them being asked to co-operate with more indepth work.

The right to grant or withhold consent presupposes the mental capacity or ability to do so. A recent report highlighted the association between competency or capacity to be well informed and the degree of previous education and doubted whether there has been sufficient recognition of the inability of some individuals to provide informed consent who have educational, social and cultural reasons that limit their understanding of complex issues.[13] You should be aware of this and act accordingly.

---

**Patients' ability to understand and consent to randomised controlled trials depends on their education[13]**

Forty middle-aged and elderly carers of patients with Alzheimer's disease (average age 64 years old) were given information about research trial design in semistructured interviews, backed by written information sheets. Three-fifths of them could not explain why placebo, randomisation and double-blind procedures were used. There was a significant positive correlation between competence to understand information about participating in a randomised controlled trial and degree of previous education received.

---

## Access to medical records

It is common to find that a researcher from outside a practice has unlimited access to patients' medical records once the GPs have pledged to co-operate in a project. This is not to suggest that such access is unduly abused but there is the potential for abuse and patients have the right to know who has access to their medical records. The sharing of information should normally only occur with a patient's consent. The Caldicott Committee report found that there was a general lack of awareness throughout the NHS of existing guidance on confidentiality and security about patients' medical details.[14]

The more that patients and the general public are involved in the delivery of healthcare, the better will be the discussion and understanding of what constitutes acceptable limits to access of patients' medical records for the purposes of professional development and the measurement of effectiveness of the services provided and performance of individual practitioners.

## Confidentiality

You should tell those you invite to participate the extent to which their identity, contact details and the information they give you are confidential to you, your work team or your organisation. If you are running a focus group or other small group work, you should suggest a code of practice to the group and seek their agreement or invite the group to decide their own rules. These will include agreement about confidentiality, exactly what information may or may not be repeated outside the group or if information may be freely repeated so long as it is not attributed to named individuals.

The Caldicott Committee report has described principles of good practice to safeguard patients' confidentiality when information is being used for non-clinical purposes.

▶ Justify the purpose.
▶ Do not use patient-identifiable information unless it is absolutely necessary.
▶ Use the minimum necessary patient-identifiable information.
▶ Access to patient-identifiable information should be on a strict need-to-know basis.
▶ Everyone with access to patient-identifiable information should be aware of their responsibilities.[14]

## Accessing and retaining participants for your consultation or survey

Before you embark on any research or consultation, you will need to think about who you want to participate in it and how you will access that group of people, get them involved and keep them interested. Some questions to ask yourself and top tips on improving access are outlined in the box below.

---

**Accessing populations and samples**

**Questions to ask yourself**
▶ Who do you want to research/consult?
▶ Will race, class and gender influence people's involvement?
▶ Can you identify any potential problems with regard to accessing this group?
▶ Who are the key consumers, carers, individuals, groups or gate-keepers, who can help you to access this group?
▶ What is the role of your initial contact, or gatekeepers, in ensuring your continuing access?
▶ Who do you need to get permission from about involvement?
▶ How much commitment will you require from the participants in terms of hours, days, weeks or months? Is this reasonable? Would you give up this amount of time for someone else?

*continued*

*continued*

**How to increase your chances of gaining access to people**

▶ Ask for advice on the most appropriate way to access the intended subjects.

▶ Be modest in your requests of people – but be open too about any further involvement they might incur after the initial contact.

▶ Make full use of your established contacts and those of your colleagues, supervisor, manager etc.

▶ Consider offering something back to your subjects, e.g. a report or a workshop.

▶ Ask people to help or participate at the right time. Be aware of busy periods etc.

▶ Be as clear as possible about what you are asking for – in terms of people, time, resources and input.

▶ Explain the reasons for doing your consultation exercise, why it will be helpful and what the outcomes might be.

▶ Minimise non-response – people who refuse to participate in your research or consultation exercises, or who initially agree, but later withdraw. Non-response can be expressed verbally or by lack of action, i.e. voting with their feet. It is not easy to address, but if you think carefully about why people might refuse before you start out, then you can make changes to make it more attractive.

## Template to evaluate the extent to which best practice was employed in undertaking a consultation exercise or survey

*1 Is there a comprehensive report of the consultation/survey?*

Check whether:

▶ it is written

▶ all stages of the consultation/survey are described; is there a stated purpose, aim, method, results, discussion, conclusions, recommendations, forward action plan?

▶ the choice of method can be justified

▶ outcome measures were specified at the start of the consultation/survey

▶ the details of the method are sufficiently full and clear that it could be duplicated if another person followed the report

▶ the results are presented in an easily understandable format. Do they seem to be complete?

▶ there is a discussion of the existence and influence of biases on the results. Is the consultation/survey set into context of previous work or others' studies elsewhere?

▶ the recommendations follow logically from the results of the consultation/survey

▶ ethical approval was sought and obtained (if appropriate)

▶ agreement was sought and obtained from host trust (if appropriate).

## 2 How biased was the consultation or survey method?

Look at the following.

▶ The extent to which the patients, citizens or groups sampled were representative of the target population. To what extent did the subjects included in the consultation/survey come from particular disease groups, locality or population rather than representing a cross-section of the population central to the question?

▶ The processes by which the citizens/subjects were involved; for example, were they sampled, elected, nominated? To what extent did everyone in the population have an equal or fair chance of being selected to take part in the consultation/survey?

▶ The response rates. Did sufficient numbers of people respond to give a reasonable chance that a full range of views was given?

▶ The distribution of age groups, gender, social class, employment status, any other important socioeconomic characteristics between respondents and non-respondents. Were the respondents representative of the whole population being consulted or surveyed?

▶ Did the consultation or survey method favour representatives with particular skills or characteristics (for example, were those without glasses or with poor communication skills less able to contribute)?

▶ Did the leader of the consultation/survey recognise the existence of particular biases in the final report?

▶ Had the leader of the consultation/survey tried to minimise the biases?

▶ Was the extent of bias resulting from the consultation/survey method acceptable?

## 3 Was the method that was set up appropriate?

Check the extent to which this was so:

▶ for the issues consulted upon

▶ for gathering responses that satisfied the purpose

▶ to match the intended outcomes

▶ for contributing patient/public opinion and views at an early enough stage in the decision-making process

▶ to gather sufficient information to know how to proceed after the consultation.

## 4 Was the information gathered used effectively?

Check if:

▶ there were any changes made from feeding results into the planning or provision of the healthcare process

▶ the target population, professionals or the authorities were consulted about the results of the consultation/survey and proposed changes to planning or provision

▶ there were any conflicts of interests (e.g. competing priorities); were they recognised, were they considered and how were they resolved?

▶ the dialogue with users, carers and the public continued after the results were published

▶ the report and results were disseminated widely to all the relevant people and organisations by appropriate means.

## 5 Was the consultation worthwhile?

Think about:

▶ whether the information was already available from other sources

▶ the realism of the resource consequences of the consultation

▶ the appropriateness of the costs of the consultation process

▶ whether the consultation process was a one-off event or part of a systematic or dynamic process

▶ whether the source of the resources used was appropriate for the purpose and outcome of the consultation/survey

▶ whether the opportunity costs arising from allocating the resources to undertake the consultation/survey were justified by the purpose and outcomes of the exercise

▶ whether there were sufficient resources to carry out a well-constructed consultation/survey or if limited resources led to cutting of corners that devalued the consultation/survey to a significant degree

▶ the extent to which the results of the consultation/survey were generalisable to other groups of people, populations, settings or circumstances.

## 6 Could the method of the consultation/survey be improved or response rate increased on a future occasion?

Consider:

▶ what facilitated or inhibited involvement of subjects in the consultation/survey and professionals or managers in undertaking the survey or implementing the recommendations that arose from the exercise

▶ what the benefits and drawbacks of involvement of patients or the public were as regards the purpose of the consultation/survey

▶ who else might have been involved to improve the information gathering and increase ownership of results and acceptance of change.

## References

1   Armstrong R and Grace J (1994) *Research Methods and Audit in General Practice*. Oxford University Press, Oxford.

2   Carter Y and Thomas C (eds) (1997) *Research Methods in Primary Care*. Radcliffe Medical Press, Oxford.

3   Blaxter L, Hughes C and Tight M (1996) *How to Research*. Open University Press, Buckingham.

4   Derry J (1993) Sample size for audit. *Managing Audit Gen Pract*. **Summer**: 17–20.

5   du Florey V (1993) Sample size for beginners. *BMJ*. **306**: 1181–4.

6   Ramsay J, Campbell J, Schroter S *et al*. (2000) The General Practice Assessment Survey (GPAS): tests of data quality and measurement properties. *Fam Pract*. **17**: 372–9.

7   Howie JGR, Heaney D, Maxwell M and Walker JJ (1998) A comparison of the Patient Enablement Instrument (PEI) against two established satisfaction scales as an outcome measure of primary care consultations. *Fam Pract*. **15**: 165–71.

8   Bower P and Roland M (2003) Bias in patient assessments of general practice: General Practice Assessment Survey scores in surgery and postal responders. *Br J Gen Pract*. **53**: 126–8.

9   The Information Commissioner, Wycliffe House, Water Lane, Wilmslow, Cheshire SK9 5AF. Tel: 01625 545745.

10  SPSS UK Ltd, SPSS House, London Street, Chertsey, KT16 8AP.

11  www.doh.gov.uk/consent

12  General Medical Council (1998) *Seeking Patients' Consent: the ethical considerations*. General Medical Council, London.

13  Pucci E, Belardinelli N and Signorino M (1999) Patients' understanding of randomised controlled trials depends on their education (letter). *BMJ*. **318**: 875.

14  Department of Health (1997) *Report on the Review of Patient-Identifiable Information (The Caldicott Committee Report)*. Department of Health, London.

## Further reading

Bowling A (1994) *Measuring Health*. Open University Press, Milton Keynes.

Calder J (1998) *Survey Research Methods*. Medical Education Booklet No. 2. Association for the Study of Medical Education (ASME), The Lister Institute, 11 Hill Square, Edinburgh EH8 9DR.

Moore D (1997) *Statistics, Concepts and Controversies* (4e). Freeman, New York.

# CHAPTER 6

# Choosing the right method for the right reasons

By now, you should know why you are involving patients and the public in healthcare and you have been introduced to the wide range of methods that people have tried with varying degrees of success. The next stage is to be able to decide which methods are the most appropriate for any particular situation.

There are four stages of thinking and preparation before you even embark on the process of involving users or engaging the public at large.

1 Take stock: be sure why you should do it at all.
2 Map out the skills and strengths of your team to assess the baseline to build on.
3 Assess the extent to which user involvement and public engagement are welcomed as a meaningful exercise by your colleagues at work. How much practical and emotional support will there be from others?
4 Before you start: define the purpose; be realistic about the magnitude of the planned exercise; select an appropriate method or several methods depending on the target population and your resources; get the commitment of everyone who will be affected by the exercise; frame the method in accordance with your perspective; write the protocol.

## Stage 1: Take stock – why do it at all?

Don't just do a survey or run a focus group because it seems a good idea or there is a requirement to do it or it will end up as a meaningless exercise at the expense of your time and needlessly raise other people's expectations about the possibility of change. So reflect on the following.

► Why are you considering organising a user involvement or public engagement exercise – what is the purpose of the exercise?
► Whose idea is it really? How many people in your practice or trust are backing the purpose of the exercise and own the initiative?

▶ Does the exercise need doing anyway? Is someone else already doing something similar and if so, can you adopt their results or tag onto their activity? Does the information already exist elsewhere that would answer the purpose of your exercise?

▶ Why are you considering being involved? Is it your job to be involved? Have you free time in which to do it or can you stop doing something else instead? Could you get someone else at your workplace to do it? Or could you get someone else from outside your workplace to do it; for example, might the clinical audit department at your trust undertake the task as part of their job or is it a responsibility that the new patients' organisations could take on?

▶ Would the exercise or activity be one part of the organisation's strategy – the business plan or the development plan? Would the task fall within a topic identified as a work-based priority or a local, district or national priority?

## Stage 2: Map out your skills and strengths for setting up a user involvement or public engagement exercise

▶ Map out the skills you have within your work team; think of what personnel might be involved and who has skills to plan the exercise, type up any survey forms, gather data, analyse data, write up the report, action the findings? Does anyone in your work team have experience of doing anything similar or relevant in the past? Is there a local university or academic department who might help with the thinking behind the planning or the execution of the exercise?

▶ Assess the enthusiasm for the exercise. Discuss the prospect at an informal staff meeting or in day-to-day contact or at a business meeting of the practice or trust to see who is likely to be co-operative.

▶ What funds do you have at your disposal? Is there any specific money available or protected staff time or has any exercise to be added as an extra to everyone's workload? Are there any patients or members of the general public who might volunteer to help without charge? When working out the costings, remember to include the opportunity costs – the work that staff will not be doing if they are participating in the exercise or carrying out a task for the project.

▶ How well organised is your practice or trust? Have you already collected information about access, availability of services, patients' usage or morbidity data that is accurate and valid? Could that information be a sound base for planning user involvement and public engagement?

▶ What structures do you already have in place for undertaking user involvement or public engagement exercises? Do you have patient or user groups? Do lay people participate in planning services, training of staff, monitoring quality or communicating information in a way that you could extend or will you be starting from scratch? Are you networking with voluntary organisations or the new patients' organisations?

▶ Are there any good models in your workplace or in neighbouring units or practices of user involvement or public engagement that include joint working between managers, clinicians, support staff and lay people on any issues that you could duplicate or from which you could learn?

▶ What is the quality of your existing patient information and education materials? Has anyone recently checked whether they are up to date, relevant and appropriate? Does the material you've got cater for people with special social or cultural needs and cover all their requirements?

## Stage 3: Do your colleagues value the patients' or public's views? Do they believe that user involvement and public engagement is a meaningful exercise?

▶ Is there a culture of wanting to establish or maintain meaningful user involvement or public engagement or do colleagues see your plans as a paper exercise?

▶ Will there be resistance from colleagues to the exercise? What will be the extent of their co-operation or active resistance to the initiative? Is it you on your own or a team or is the drive to engage in this work coming from the organisation?

▶ Are the advantages to be gained from public engagement or user involvement clear to you and your colleagues?

▶ Are you and your colleagues aware of the drawbacks of public engagement or user involvement in respect of your particular planned exercise(s)?

▶ What are your and other colleagues' expectations of the usefulness of any exercise? Do you/they have positive expectations and anticipate the exercise leading to useful improvements? Or do you/they expect negative outcomes such as increasing patient demands or the staff workload?

▶ Do you or other colleagues have preconceived views about the willingness or ability of your patient population or the general community to co-operate and participate in user involvement or public engagement exercises? Do you/they have preferences for the population groups with which you prefer to work? Will there be any prejudices to overcome or difficulties to surmount amongst the staff – social, cultural, educational, lifestyle, etc?

# Stage 4:  How to start – making it happen

▶ Agree the purpose of the exercise with all your colleagues at work who will be affected by the exercise – either in the planning, organising, gathering of data, affording the costs, using the findings, working with the users or the general public, publicising the exercise or outcomes, etc.

▶ Define the question or the purpose of your exercise. Is it about:
  – improving information or communication or establishing people's preferences?
  – making difficult decisions about funding or resources; rationing or prioritising services; changing the availability of services, personnel or premises?
  – clinical governance; monitoring or improving the quality of clinical care or services?
  – assessing and targeting needs; containing demand?

▶ Be realistic in your choice of method depending on whether:
  – you have identified resources: skills, practical support, people, time, money, experience, enthusiasm
  – your practice or organisation and colleagues are behind you
  – you are capitalising on momentum created by the strategy at work or it being a priority
  – you are building on successful previous initiatives.

▶ Select an appropriate method for the population concerned:
  – the whole practice population or local community (users and non-users of your healthcare services)
  – identifiable patient groups
  – individual patients, carers or families.

▶ Frame the method depending on whether the exercise is to be from the perspective of:
  – a strategic health authority or locality
  – a primary care trust or hospital trust
  – a practice, department or clinic
  – an individual practitioner or member of staff.

▶ Write down the protocol for the exercise to include:
  – the purpose
  – the target population
  – the chosen method: how to sample or recruit lay people and professionals, the details of all the stages of the method – where, when, how many, who will do what
  – how other colleagues will be involved: how they will participate or how you will keep them informed and motivated
  – any training needs or skill deficits: how these will be addressed
  – the timetable
  – expected outcomes
  – resources, anticipated budget including time, staff, costs

- context of the exercise: whether it is a one-off event or part of a programme of involvement/engagement or a preliminary stage to further work
- method of evaluation
- anticipated changes: possible alternatives that are realistic, acceptable, appropriate
- expected dissemination: how you will feedback the outcomes of the exercise to the target population, those who participated in the exercise, the community at large, your work team, the strategic health authority, etc.

► Arrange educational programmes as necessary for (i) those working in primary and community healthcare and the voluntary sector and (ii) members of the public, users and carers to learn how to initiate or participate in lay consultation/involvement, to make the most of resources or opportunities and use the results of the consultation effectively.

# Stage 5: Involving patients and the public appropriately

Use the lists of alternatives below to help you decide what method(s) you will use. There are many varied examples to illustrate the sort of objectives, topics or themes for the type of patient or general public populations with which you might work. The objectives, topics, populations and methods described are by no means comprehensive, they are just intended to give you examples of the kind of approaches you should consider. Your own circumstances will limit your choice of methods for all the reasons previously listed above. The characteristics of your local population and the quality of the current provision of services will shape your purpose and the subsidiary objectives of the patient or public information and involvement activities on which you embark; they may be completely different from any illustrated here.

Refer back to the previous chapters for descriptions of the different types of involvement and engagement exercises, their relative advantages and drawbacks and how to carry them out. If you are uncertain of how to proceed, get help from others who have done similar exercises before rather than waste time and effort on an exercise that is set up badly.

The section that follows lays out your pathways of choices. Start with the purpose – four main areas are given as examples.

► Improve information or communication for patients and the public to take account of their preferences.
► Make difficult decisions about treatment, funding or resources.
► Implement clinical governance.
► Assess and target needs within the limits of resources.

You may find that the purpose of *your* intended user involvement or public engagement exercise overlaps into several different areas; just look at each relevant section and choose methods that might suit more than one purpose or use a method from each. For each purpose, several specific objectives are listed but you might frame others more pertinent to your situation or that are more urgent for you to resolve. Several examples follow that describe typical topics that practices and trusts often identify as problem areas or sources of friction between the services and NHS care that they provide and patients' and the public's perspectives of what they want or receive.

Suggestions for alternative methods you might select are given according to whether you are considering the user involvement or public engagement exercise from a population perspective – your practice, district or local community – or from the perspective of an identifiable patient group or individuals within that group – elderly people, those with disabilities, carers of those with dementia, etc. From there, the choice of methods is further subdivided into whether you want to 'interact' with the users or the public so that there is a two-way exchange of information or mainly want to 'receive' or to 'give' information. When you are considering how to involve the 'general public' or your whole 'patient population', at least one of your chosen methods will need to be a way of interacting with 'non-users' as well as 'users'; whilst if you intend to involve 'identifiable patient groups', they should be more straightforward to reach.

Don't forget, these methods are not a choice between one or another as any involvement or opinion exercise will be more valid if you obtain views and input from more than one source to minimise bias. So if you are considering an important topic and want wide-ranging views, choose two or three different methods, put the results together and compare your findings. For health needs assessment, you should think of involving the public and patients in the three approaches of gaining information about effectiveness, population data and services.

Don't cut corners because you do not have sufficient resources to undertake the user involvement exercise properly, so that you leave out essential stages like piloting questionnaires, using a convenience sample of people rather than a random sample or omitting the briefing session before one of the consensus methods. The reasons why you should keep to the standard scientific methods were explained in Chapter 5 and if you sacrifice best practice for expediency, you will devalue your exercise if your users are biased or too few and the outcome will be meaningless. If you do not have enough resources or skills, either wait until you have rectified the deficiency or select another method that you can afford or have the ability to undertake.

▼
Appropriate patient involvement.

# How to do it – alternative pathways to user and public involvement

*1 Purpose: To improve information or communication for patients or the general public and take account of their preferences*

**Possible specific objectives**

- ▶ To find out what particular groups of patients want, if the quality of information and communication is good enough, if the information is accessible, if it is in a suitable format.
- ▶ To ascertain users' and non-users' views about the quality of information, the readability, contents, level of information of strategy documents or patient education materials.
- ▶ To assess whether particular patient groups have more problems with information or communication than others.
- ▶ To determine patients' expectations, preferences, needs – for access, range of services, personnel delivering care, responsiveness.
- ▶ To establish the preferences of lay people about the provision of health services and the management of medical conditions.
- ▶ To determine what levels of side effects or adverse consequences patients find acceptable when choosing to take up new or alternative treatments.
- ▶ To limit access to patients' medical records to the members of the multidisciplinary team that patients and the general public find acceptable.
- ▶ To find out whether patients are generally satisfied with the opportunities they have for consulting the health professionals of their choice.

**Examples of topics you might consider**

- ▶ Literature for patients undergoing tests. You might involve people in saying what they want, if the literature is accurate or detailed enough, if it is written in words with which patients are familiar, with a good balance between illustrations and text.
- ▶ The range of information for elderly people. You might find out how those who are hard of hearing, visually impaired or suffer from dementia currently fare and what they want in the way of written, pictorial, audiocassette, large print or video alternatives.
- ▶ The range and effectiveness of communication of health promotion messages to hard-to-reach groups, such as the homeless, gypsies/travellers, young men. Are messages reaching them in an appropriate way at the right time? Are the messages understood, do they make an impact and do changes in behaviour result?
- ▶ Strategy documents such as the Local Delivery Plan. You might involve people in defining priorities, planning how to present the

*Purpose: To improve information or communication for patients or the general public and take account of their preferences*

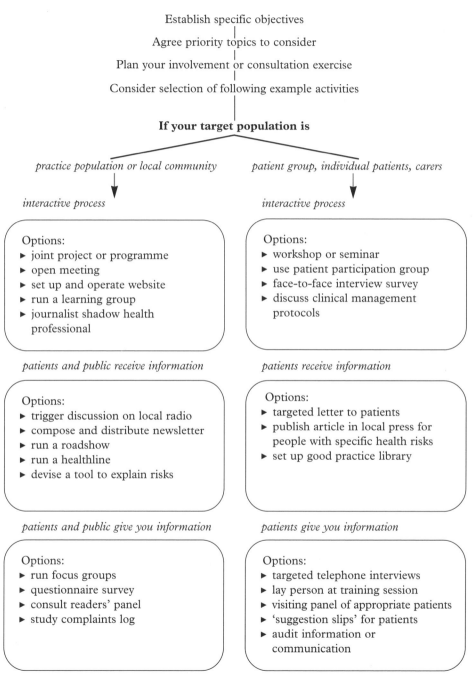

Establish specific objectives

Agree priority topics to consider

Plan your involvement or consultation exercise

Consider selection of following example activities

**If your target population is**

*practice population or local community*          *patient group, individual patients, carers*

*interactive process*                              *interactive process*

Options:
▶ joint project or programme
▶ open meeting
▶ set up and operate website
▶ run a learning group
▶ journalist shadow health
   professional

Options:
▶ workshop or seminar
▶ use patient participation group
▶ face-to-face interview survey
▶ discuss clinical management
   protocols

*patients and public receive information*          *patients receive information*

Options:
▶ trigger discussion on local radio
▶ compose and distribute newsletter
▶ run a roadshow
▶ run a healthline
▶ devise a tool to explain risks

Options:
▶ targeted letter to patients
▶ publish article in local press for
   people with specific health risks
▶ set up good practice library

*patients and public give you information*          *patients give you information*

Options:
▶ run focus groups
▶ questionnaire survey
▶ consult readers' panel
▶ study complaints log

Options:
▶ targeted telephone interviews
▶ lay person at training session
▶ visiting panel of appropriate patients
▶ 'suggestion slips' for patients
▶ audit information or
   communication

messages, monitoring and implementing the plans or commenting on the contents of a draft version as to its relevance and readability.

▶ Health professionals' access to sources of evidence-based information and communication of that knowledge to patients; or direct access for lay people to similar sources.

▶ Alternative treatments for various cancers – patients' information needs, doctors' communication skills, the trust's or practice's communication record.

▶ Patients' perceptions of risks or side effects of long-term treatments for various chronic illnesses.

▶ Patients' preferences for complementary and traditional therapies.

▶ Patients' satisfaction with their choice of gender, ethnicity or age of their usual or the latest doctor, nurse or therapist consulted.

▶ Ethnic differences such as different perceptions and expectations of health and illness.

**Possible approach using one or several methods, depending on the purpose of the exercise and the available resources**

*If your target population is the whole practice population or local community*

and you want to use an **interactive process for patients and the public to give and receive** information

▶ Operate joint working: joint managerial/lay/clinical input into a local project or programme.

▶ Hold an open meeting at the practice or trust with plenty of opportunities for discussion.

▶ Set up and operate your own website, advertising the availability of services, giving health messages and encouraging discussion or feedback; questions might be posed by the public for professionals to answer.

▶ Join a learning group (sometimes known as learner set, learning set, action learner set) of health and social care professionals and lay people set up as an educational activity where participants come to understand more about each others' constraints, capabilities, roles and responsibilities. The exercise will have most effect if the participants are relatively senior and can stimulate cultural changes in their own work setting, in response to their learning.

▶ Invite a journalist to spend time observing medical practice. Health professionals and the journalist will learn from each other and the learning will be subsequently passed onto the general lay readership.

or you want patients and the public to **receive** information from you

▶ Publish articles in the local press.

▶ Trigger a discussion topic on the local radio – send in a story, participate in a phone-in session, give an interview.

▶ Compose your own newsletter and distribute it to the local community or place it at public access points.

▶ Display posters in your waiting room which are informative and individualised for your practice or trust, describing topical matters.

▶ Run a roadshow with demonstrations of anything related to good information and communication systems or initiatives – perhaps in schools, community centres.

▶ Run a healthline at district level or dedicated phone-in time for general health information at the general practice level. Link or refer to NHS Direct or other national helplines as appropriate.

▶ Devise a tool (or use someone else's) to explain the risks of various treatment options to patients derived from published literature, comparing their risks with easily understandable risks in everyday life (for instance, being killed in a car accident).

or you want patients and the public to **give** you information

▶ Run focus groups involving representatives of particular groups of patients.

▶ Carry out a questionnaire survey:
 – general: e.g. in a newspaper or attached to a strategy document circulated to the public
 – targeted: as a postal survey or semistructured interviews, e.g. to special interest groups, user groups, key people
 – research study: for example, weighting of risks or views about alternative treatments. When results are disseminated in a journal, a wider population will be reached if the author writes short articles about the findings for the lay press.

▶ Consult a readers' panel: recruit a lay group to 'read' and give constructive feedback on draft business plans, strategy documents, etc.

▶ Study complaints: log verbal informal complaints and do an indepth review of relatively minor complaints and then act on the lessons by changing systems and practice.

▶ Invite patients to log on to your practice's or trust's website and leave suggestions or comments.

*If your target population is an identifiable patient group or individual patients or carers within that group*

and you want to use an **interactive process for patients to give and receive** information

▶ Hold a workshop or seminar – do joint work in small groups. Rewrite information material for patients or delegate task to a lay writer.

▶ Use your patient participation group. Practice or trust staff might attend for an agenda item of joint interest to hear and explain each other's viewpoints.

▶ Carry out a face-to-face interview survey of a target population group in the course of routine work (for example, when visiting the housebound) by staff using a structured or semistructured interview schedule.

▶ Discuss clinical management protocols or guidelines with patients, such as via a computerised decision support system, where associated education leaflets in-form and enable patients to participate in the decision making.

or you want patients to **receive** information from you

▶ Send a targeted letter to patients with a particular problem, giving them an update of newly published evidence, for instance.

▶ Ask patients who have had particularly pertinent or 'ordinary' experiences of different treatment alternatives to write short accounts or tell their stories taped onto audiocassettes, to share with patients coming after them. Keep a database of such experienced patients prepared to telephone others newly presenting with the same problem, who need to speak to someone who has had a recent similar experience. Involve any trainees or students in the exercise.

▶ Set up a good practice library of patient educational materials from which to lend books, videos, CD-ROMs and audiocassettes to appropriate patients. Some commercial companies sponsor non-promotional material designed to inform patients about the symptoms, signs and risks of their illness and encourage compliance with treatment.

▶ Publish articles in local press for lay readers with specific health risks such as smokers, those who are overweight or who are at risk of sexual diseases.

or you want patients to **give** you information

▶ Carry out a questionnaire survey. The method will depend on the characteristics of the patient group and if there are any social, cultural, language or ability limitations – use a postal survey or a telephone interview to targeted patients.

▶ Organise a training session with a lay person as one of the session's 'teachers' helping health professionals to understand the patient's perspective and why problems arise, such as non-compliance or disruptive behaviour.

▶ Set up an evaluation of a particular aspect of care or services that your practice or trust offers, by arranging for a visiting panel of appropriate patients or representatives of the public to assess the services with respect to the range, quality or difficulties of access.

▶ Attach 'suggestion slips' to repeat prescriptions or appointment letters of patients with particular conditions inviting their input about anything related to their care or specifically enquiring about an aspect of the service.

▶ Undertake an audit of an important aspect of the quality of information or communication. Involve lay people in setting the criteria and standards, reviewing performance compared to standards, discussing the changes.

▶ Run focus groups of patients with a particular experience. But beware members of users' groups who have become too polished at relaying their histories, for whom too much time has elapsed since the relevant experience for them to remember clearly the emotions and thoughts they had at the time.

## 2 Purpose: To make difficult decisions about treatment, funding or resources

**Possible specific objectives**

▶ To gain people's views about how decisions about rationing or prioritising services or treatments should be made, who should be involved and when.

▶ To review what factors should be considered when prioritising a health problem as regards the allocation of resources.

▶ To centralise services and reduce peripheral facilities.

▶ To take an overview about whether resources are allocated according to need between health and social care sectors or between health and education sectors.

▶ To look at reducing costs by using less skilled staff for the aspect of care under consideration; and if the skill mix is changed, to determine whether less skilled staff do actually cost less in the long run.

▶ To help patients share in decision making about alternative treatment options in informed and meaningful ways.

▶ To find out what services patients or the general public think the NHS should provide for particular groups of people.

▶ To determine people's views before a new procedure is brought in, to understand their information needs and afterwards to learn from their experiences.

**Examples of topics you might consider**

▶ Agree local criteria for funding non-life-saving medical treatments such as fertility treatments.

▶ Substitute nurses for doctors, assistants for qualified therapists, counsellors for psychologists to provide healthcare services.

▶ Review funding arrangements, responsibilities of staff in health and social care organisations for bathing elderly people at home or providing aids for people with disabilities.

*Purpose:  To make difficult decisions about treatment, funding or resources*

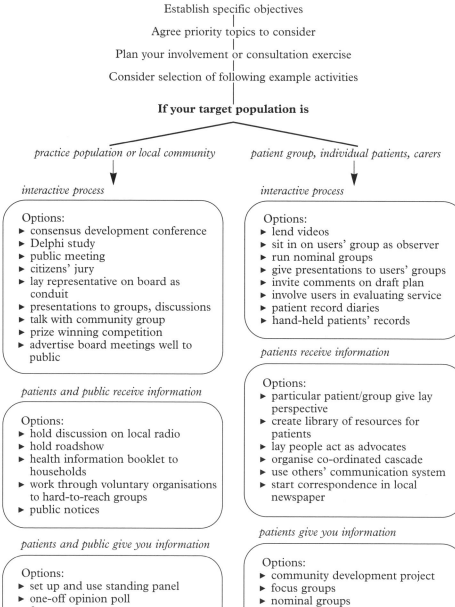

Establish specific objectives

Agree priority topics to consider

Plan your involvement or consultation exercise

Consider selection of following example activities

**If your target population is**

*practice population or local community*

*patient group, individual patients, carers*

*interactive process*

Options:
► consensus development conference
► Delphi study
► public meeting
► citizens' jury
► lay representative on board as conduit
► presentations to groups, discussions
► talk with community group
► prize winning competition
► advertise board meetings well to public

*patients and public receive information*

Options:
► hold discussion on local radio
► hold roadshow
► health information booklet to households
► work through voluntary organisations to hard-to-reach groups
► public notices

*patients and public give you information*

Options:
► set up and use standing panel
► one-off opinion poll
► focus groups
► semistructured interviews
► neighbourhood forums
► rapid appraisal initiative

*interactive process*

Options:
► lend videos
► sit in on users' group as observer
► run nominal groups
► give presentations to users' groups
► invite comments on draft plan
► involve users in evaluating service
► patient record diaries
► hand-held patients' records

*patients receive information*

Options:
► particular patient/group give lay perspective
► create library of resources for patients
► lay people act as advocates
► organise co-ordinated cascade
► use others' communication system
► start correspondence in local newspaper

*patients give you information*

Options:
► community development project
► focus groups
► nominal groups
► face-to-face interviews
► feedback or evaluation slips

► Agree if and what social, age, lifestyle and prognostic criteria might be applied to limit people's entitlement to expensive treatments such as kidney transplantation or cardiac surgery.

► The extent of patients' choice with respect to referral for a medical opinion or treatment outside the district.

► How investment decisions should be made with regard to reducing waiting lists for treatment; weighing resources for the treatment of potentially life-threatening against treatment for incapacitating but non-life-threatening conditions.

► Gauging views about whether people with acute eye problems would consult an optometrist instead of a GP or the A&E department and if such a service is acceptable, how should access be arranged and should users pay a fee?

► Patients' and the public's views on whether complementary therapy should be available as part of NHS treatment and if so, which therapies should be included?

► Changing surgery opening hours.

**Possible approach using one or several methods, depending on the purpose of the exercise and the available resources**

*If your target population is the whole practice population or local community*

and you want to use an **interactive process for patients and the public to give and receive** information and opinions about making difficult decisions

► Run a consensus development conference with a mix of professionals and lay people.

► Consider a Delphi study of key leaders in the locality.

► See if your overarching organisation – the trust, health authority or central NHS Executive – will help look after your interests by organising a co-ordinated and equitable approach to the difficult decision. They will have more resources for obtaining a wider cross-section of views and exchanging information with the local community.

► Organise a public consultation meeting.

► Set up a citizens' jury, briefed well, to consider the issues and prioritise different action plans.

► Ask the lay representative(s) on the trust board to serve as a conduit for a two-way exchange of information with their networks with the public.

► Make presentations to groups with particular interests or responsibilities for the subject in question, with plenary discussions.

► Feedback and exchange information with a community group, who may conduct their own consultation.

► Compose public notices or published articles setting out the issues and proposals and inviting comments, either in answer to structured questions or as free comments.

▶ Run a competition with a small prize for people who send in the best name for the planned new venture – that should attract more people's notice – and give you an opportunity to explain the rationale for the planned changes and invite comments at the same time.

▶ Advertise the board meetings of the trust well to the public. Make the lay or staff audience feel welcome and invite them to participate.

or you want patients and the public to **receive** information and opinions about making difficult decisions

▶ Interest the media in holding a discussion on the topic on the local radio; participate in a phone-in session, contribute to a debate and give an interview to explain the issues.

▶ Hold a roadshow, presenting the issues and describing the alternatives. Give anonymised examples from real life so that people can understand how the limited resources affect people's way of life or well-being.

▶ Deliver health information booklet to all households advising about appropriate action to take for medical problems, using patients' representatives to help with the distribution.

▶ Use voluntary organisations and their contacts and networks to communicate with hard-to-reach groups of the population.

▶ Submit articles to the press. Try and interest the press sufficiently so that they send a photographer along; the picture will capture people's attention more effectively than text.

or you want patients and the public to **give** you information and opinions about making difficult decisions

▶ Set up and use a standing panel or consult the population using someone else's panel. Has your local authority set up a standing citizens' panel that you could tag onto for health matters?

▶ Commission opinion poll by market research company in the street or by telephone.

▶ Run focus groups but you might want to avoid patients or their families directly suffering as a result of limited resources to treat the condition or circumstances at issue, if you want considered opinions as opposed to an emotional wrangle.

▶ Look for other models outside the health service where the public inform difficult decision making and see if their approach is feasible for you.

▶ Carry out semistructured interviews with senior members of community, key opinion leaders, etc.

▶ Contact neighbourhood forums and ask them to debate the issues at their next meetings. Make a regular arrangement with a local forum so that you can each select an item for the other's agenda and feedback views.

▶ Organise a rapid appraisal initiative. Use a mix of community development approaches for a snapshot of all the different types of information known about the issue in a particular community and talk to key people to find out their views.

▶ Carry out a literature search or ask around; has anyone tried what you are proposing elsewhere? Phone up contacts and discuss the pros and cons of how their new services or changes are working out. Learn from them and generalise their experiences to your situation if you can.

*If your target population is an identifiable patient group or individual patients or carers within that group*

and you want to use an **interactive process for patients to give and receive** information and opinions about making difficult decisions

▶ Lend a video to an individual patient with a serious condition for which a difficult decision must be made. Or find other educational material (see Appendix) that is appropriate to what they want and need to know about their options. Once they are well informed, you will be able to share the decision making in a more meaningful way.

▶ Sit in on a users' group as an observer; it will soon become an interactive exchange as the users make the most of the opportunity to ask you questions and you hear their concerns and can discuss decision making about difficult issues!

▶ Run nominal groups with interested organisations.

▶ Organise presentations to particular users' groups by someone at the centre with a grasp of the issues, followed by an interactive discussion. Explain advantages of the planned changes over the current system.

▶ Send a draft plan to a voluntary group or a patients' group and ask for comments or ask them to plan out how they will implement your proposal.

▶ Set up a pilot project and involve users and staff in evaluating how well the new service or arrangements work at every stage. Be prepared to revise or discard such an initiative if it is rated as unpopular or ineffective.

▶ Use record diaries to allow patients to log the frequency and magnitude of their symptoms prospectively over a month or longer; this should trigger the advice and information they really want from the doctor, nurse or therapist at the next consultation.

▶ Introduce and evaluate the use of patient-held records for a chronic medical condition. Such records should improve shared decision making as the patient is kept up to date with their current management, enabling them to reflect on future options before the associated decision has to be taken.

or you want patients to **receive** information and opinions about making difficult decisions

▶ Arrange for others who have suffered the same problem to talk to a particular patient or patient group to give their lay perspectives of the alternatives available.

▶ Arrange for one or more carers who have made difficult decisions in the past to talk to a carer or group of carers who are having problems with the person they are caring for. Join the discussion and learn at first hand how people make such decisions so that you have more understanding in the future.

▶ Create a practice or trust library of resources where patients can borrow appropriate books, tapes and videos to inform them about the issues to consider when making their own critical decisions.

▶ Recruit lay people to act as advocates for patients who are fazed by authority or intellectually unable to take their own decisions, to befriend such patients and help them make rational decisions about treatment options.

▶ Organise a co-ordinated cascade system for passing on information, via staff or representatives of patients' groups.

▶ Display warning notices about any planned changes several weeks before the changes occur to get people familiar with the new systems; write a simple information leaflet describing the planned changes and giving a timetable of events.

▶ Piggyback onto some other organisation's communication system. Next time they are sending circulars to particular patients or groups, add a memo or letter from you to their correspondence.

▶ Write a letter to the local newspaper – many individual patients will read that. Ask people to tell others about the issues in your letter and contact you if they wish.

<u>or you want patients to</u> **give** <u>you information and opinions about making difficult decisions</u>

▶ Use a community development project that is already established to gather information about the issue. Ask appropriate people at your local health promotion department or city council what community development is taking place.

▶ Ask a patient who has made a difficult decision about treatment options how they might have been helped more or been better informed.

▶ Run focus groups, perhaps of carers or patients with a condition relevant to the planned change.

▶ Organise nominal groups of people involved in providing the changes – health and social care professionals – and those receiving care or representing those who do – lay people, as unidisciplinary or mixed groups.

▶ Carry out face-to-face interviews or make a simple enquiry of the individual patients or carers most likely to be affected. Interviews might be carried out by able lay people from a voluntary organisation, for example.

▶ Give out or administer simple feedback or evaluation slips for people using the pilot or current service that you plan to change, inviting views about current standards, wants and needs. Try to arrange the enquiry so that responses are anonymous and non-identifable to encourage people to give honest replies.

## 3 Purpose: To implement clinical governance

**Background**

> Clinical governance has been defined as 'a framework through which NHS organisations are accountable for continuously improving the quality of their services, safeguarding high standards by creating an environment in which excellence in clinical care will flourish'.[1]

**Possible specific objectives**

> ► To monitor or improve the quality of selected examples of clinical care or aspects of services.
> ► To find out whether there are any problems with access to care for different patient groups and where access might be improved.
> ► To assess the quality of care of a medical condition with regard to diagnosis, investigation, clinical and organisational management.
> ► To determine the quality of interpersonal relationships between all the health professionals and support staff with whom particular patients come into contact.
> ► To look from the patient's perspective at whether NHS staff have appropriate skills, attitudes and knowledge with respect to providing healthcare for specific medical conditions.
> ► To explore whether doctors and nurses explain evidence-based or best practice of clinical management in ways that convince patients so that they comply with recommended treatment regimes.

**Examples of topics you might consider**

> ► Prescribing patterns and adherence to agreed prescribing policies.
> ► Access for the disabled to premises and toilets and when climbing up onto an examination couch.
> ► Conforming of practitioners' chronic disease management to agreed evidence-based management protocols.
> ► Quality of consultation from patient's point of view – health professional listens, explains, appears technically competent, gives clear advice and instructions, shares decisions.
> ► Risk management policies exist and are applied, for example in the rapid response to patients presenting with life-threatening emergencies.
> ► An objective educational assessment of clinical and support staff's capabilities to undertake patient information or public involvement activities in a meaningful way. Design an educational programme to rectify gaps in knowledge, attitudes and skills.

*Purpose: To implement clinical governance*

Establish specific objectives

Agree priority topics to consider

Plan your involvement or consultation exercise

Consider selection of following example activities

**If your target population is**

*practice population or local community*          *patient group, individual patients, carers*

*interactive process*                             *interactive process*

Options:
▶ run seminar for users and carers
▶ standing panel
▶ bulletin board on website

Options:
▶ presentation to patients' groups
▶ patient participation group comment
▶ register for higher award of quality
▶ design information leaflets for particular groups

*patients receive information*

*patients and public receive information*

Options:
▶ newsletter describing standards
▶ present comparative information about prescribing patterns
▶ submit article to local press

Options:
▶ information leaflets for particular groups
▶ patients' 'mini-charters' of best practice
▶ summary of news to patients, carers

*patients give you information*

*patients and public give you information*

Options:
▶ audit telephone access
▶ visiting panel of lay people
▶ track numbers of patients
▶ focus groups

Options:
▶ disabled person in wheelchair looks round your premises
▶ focus group of users
▶ focus groups of carers
▶ lay input into training sessions

**Possible approach using one or several methods, depending on the purpose of the exercise and the available resources**

*If your target population is the whole practice population or local community*

and you want to use an **interactive process for patients and the public to give and receive** input about the implementing of clinical governance

▸ Run a seminar for users and carers and representatives of voluntary organisations to explain the meaning, issues and implications of clinical governance; invite informed patients and the public to participate in a second seminar with clinicians and managers to agree priorities for a clinical governance development programme.

▸ Use a standing panel to establish concerns and priorities about the quality of care and services to be addressed under the clinical governance umbrella.

▸ Create a Patient's Charter after preliminary qualitative work with patients' groups to establish what rights all, or a particular group of, patients can realistically expect and what responsibilities those patients should assume. Monitor the extent to which the Charter standards are met, by involving a visiting lay panel or the lay representative on the trust board, the Patients' Forum or other patients' representatives.

▸ Advertise a bulletin board on your website for news and discussion about standards of healthcare in the practice or trust.

or you want patients and the public to **receive** feedback or news about the implementing of clinical governance

▸ Publish a newsletter describing the standards of care your practice or trust aspires to or reached recently.

▸ Present identifiable comparative information about prescribing patterns at a public board meeting with the agreement of the clinicians (*note*: this idea might be better placed in the 'interactive' category as you are bound to trigger a lot of discussion and debate by releasing such sensitive information).

▸ Submit an article to the local press about the success of a recent initiative or new services that have been established.

or you want patients and the public to **give** you input about the implementing of clinical governance

▸ Audit telephone access: find out from the telephone company what proportion of callers find the line engaged at peak periods. Ask patients to comment on whether the standards of telephone access achieved are acceptable.

▸ Ask a visiting panel of lay people to comment on access to your premises, then invite them to reassess the situation after you have made improvements.

► Track a specific number of patients with the medical problems you are studying and ask them to report prospectively on their experiences at stages in their care pathway from primary care to secondary care and the parallel treatment by staff in both sectors. Ask about various aspects of the quality of care they received. Discuss the results at a management meeting.

► Organise focus groups – of patients with same condition.

► Consider feedback from Patients' Forum or Patient Advice and Liaison Service (PALS).

*If your target population is an identifiable patient group or individual patients or carers within that group*

<u>and you want to use an</u> **interactive process with patients, carers and non-users to give and receive** <u>input about implementing clinical governance</u>

► Make a presentation to particular patients' groups by GPs, nurses or managers, followed by opportunities for discussion and exchange of views.

► Invite your patient participation group to comment on your practice developmental plan in detail; arrange equal numbers of lay people and key members of the practice team. Facilitate interactive exchange where people are free to give constructive comments without fear.

▼

**Lay input into training sessions can be valuable.**

▶ Register for a higher award of quality,[2] such as Investors in People, the British Standards Institution ISO 9000 scheme, the Charter Mark scheme or the Royal College of General Practitioners' Fellowship by Assessment; the interaction that results will not only include review and discussion of the quality and purpose of staff training but will require two-way interchanges with users, carers and non-users on audit, effectiveness and all aspects of the organisation.

▶ Design information leaflets for particular groups with the help of some of their members to give essential information; for example, leaflets to catch adolescents' attention about the availability of emergency contraception will benefit from a youngster advising on the content and presentation. Attaching a comment slip with freepost address on the reverse side might attract suggestions for meeting their needs – time, place, personnel, etc.

or you want patients, carers and non-users to **receive** input about implementing clinical governance from you

▶ Design information leaflets for particular groups as for the interactive exchange above but without feedback slips; target elderly people, youngsters.

▶ Give patients 'mini-charters' listing best practice in the management of their chronic conditions so that they can compare the management they receive against this information. The information about best practice might come from decision support systems, self-help associations, an Internet site or be derived from the National Institute of Clinical Effectiveness (NICE) guidelines or the National Service Frameworks (NSFs).

▶ Send a short summary of news about your activities that come under the clinical governance umbrella to secretaries of key patient, carer and professional groups or organisations from other sectors such as schools or day centres; keep them informed about your improvement programme and how they might get involved. Include groups and their representatives whom you have never thought of writing to before but who contribute to the provision of healthcare locally. This should have the additional benefit of encouraging networking and joint working and reducing duplication of initiatives.

or you want patients, carers and non-users to **give** you input about implementing clinical governance

▶ Take a disabled person in a wheelchair round your premises into every part where you would expect an able-bodied patient to have access. Ask them to point out the difficulties and impossibilities and give you ideas on ways to overcome the problems.

▶ Set up a focus group of users: for example, to debate access and availability of services or discuss the usual reception they experience from staff.

▶ Run a focus group with carers: for example, to debate the availability of home visits, response to out-of-hours requests for medical care, provision of equipment and aids, continuity of care from multi-disciplinary team.

▶ Arrange lay input into training sessions of support staff and clinicians, to encourage training to be relevant to patients' needs.

▶ Consider feedback from others' reviews such as those of the Commission for Healthcare Audit and Inspection (CHAI).

## 4 Purpose: To assess and target needs appropriately within the limits of resources

### Background

The ten steps of health needs assessment are:

1 understand your population
2 identify the incidence and prevalence of the condition or problem
3 calculate the expected number of cases
4 measure service utilisation
5 calculate unmet needs
6 review effectiveness of interventions
7 seek population's views
8 find out professionals' views
9 agree priorities
10 define interventions and healthcare programmes.[3,4]

That is, health needs assessment encompasses the potential to benefit from care (need), expressed desire for services (demand) and services that are actually provided in relation to need or demand (supply). Health needs assessment includes epidemiological, comparative, corporate and qualitative approaches with 'macro' population or 'micro' patient-based perspectives.

### Possible specific objectives

▶ To draw up a profile of the local population, including the structure, environment, lifestyles, culture and religions, measures of disease and disability.

▶ To identify the needs of the whole community, particular patient groups or individual patients that are not (fully) addressed by current services.

▶ To contain demand for services at levels commensurate with current resources.

▶ To determine whether any particular patient groups are discriminated against or in other ways disadvantaged by current ways of planning and delivering NHS services.

▶ To look at the quality of care according to several or all of Maxwell's dimensions of quality, namely: efficiency and economy, effectiveness

*Purpose: To assess and target needs appropriately within the limits of resources*

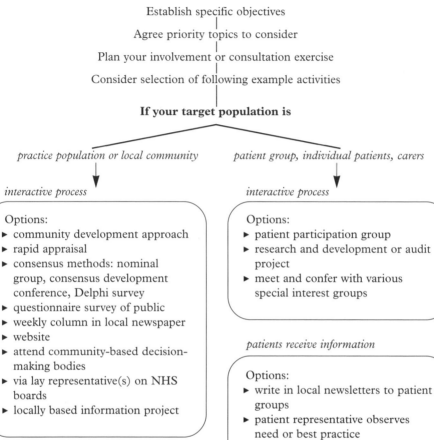

Establish specific objectives

Agree priority topics to consider

Plan your involvement or consultation exercise

Consider selection of following example activities

**If your target population is**

*practice population or local community*

*patient group, individual patients, carers*

*interactive process*

Options:
- ▸ community development approach
- ▸ rapid appraisal
- ▸ consensus methods: nominal group, consensus development conference, Delphi survey
- ▸ questionnaire survey of public
- ▸ weekly column in local newspaper
- ▸ website
- ▸ attend community-based decision-making bodies
- ▸ via lay representative(s) on NHS boards
- ▸ locally based information project

*interactive process*

Options:
- ▸ patient participation group
- ▸ research and development or audit project
- ▸ meet and confer with various special interest groups

*patients receive information*

Options:
- ▸ write in local newsletters to patient groups
- ▸ patient representative observes need or best practice
- ▸ contact particular population group for informal 'chat'
- ▸ employ support worker as link to patient group

*patients and public receive information*

Options:
- ▸ newspaper articles
- ▸ local radio: health promotion
- ▸ targeted health promotion for hard-to-reach groups

*patients give you information*

Options:
- ▸ focus groups
- ▸ interviews
- ▸ comment slips for patients
- ▸ undertake library search
- ▸ health parliament

*patients and public give you information*

Options:
- ▸ questionnaire survey
- ▸ poster campaign
- ▸ comment slips for the public

(for individual patients), relevance to need (for the whole community), social acceptability, equity and access to services, with respect to all of the district population or subsections of the community.[5]

▶ To consider fair ways of weighting resources between different practices or subgroups of the population in a PCT population, for various aspects of patient care.

▶ To compare the different approaches of social services, the strategic health authority, a PCT and community nurses to health needs assessments and determine whether any way is more effective than another for reaching and involving particular patient populations.

▶ To determine the most effective interventions for particular conditions.

**Examples of topics you might consider**

▶ Out-of-hours care: assess the quality of provision of out-of-hours medical care at trust or practice levels or from the health authority perspective across the district.

▶ Any of the objectives for patients with particular characteristics such as adolescents, young mothers, elderly people, employed people whose working hours restrict their access to medical care, people without a car or telephone.

▶ Any of the objectives for people with particular needs such as those with a learning disability, people with severe mental health problems, the homeless, deprived communities such as those in remote rural areas or the inner cities.

▶ The needs of various ethnic groups with respect to known ethnic differences such as different disease patterns, different cultures, racism and discrimination, lack of involvement in planning and organisation of their health services.[3]

▶ Assessment of needs and provision of services for housebound people: carers who find difficulty leaving their charges, people with profound disabilities, those who are terminally ill.

**Possible approach using one or several methods, depending on the purpose of the exercise and the available resources**

*If your target population is the whole practice population or local community*

and you want to use an **interactive process for patients and the public to give and receive** information and advice about assessing and targeting patients' or the general public's needs

▶ Adopt a community development approach: co-ordinate or work through the community development workers, health promotion facilitators, health visitors, social workers, employees and volunteers in the non-statutory sector who are already in post.

▶ Use rapid appraisal: involve health professionals, social workers and others to encourage ownership of findings and eventual solutions. Hold further discussions with the general public when the findings are published whilst evolving and deciding on the best solutions.

▶ Employ a consensus method: nominal group, consensus development conference, Delphi survey – depending on how wide ranging the topic is.

▶ Undertake a questionnaire survey of the general public: place in a newspaper or attach to a strategy document such as the Local Delivery Plan (this is in a *give and receive* category because such a questionnaire would be attached to a newspaper article or document describing the plans and discussing the issues).

▶ Speak in a local radio discussion programme or phone-in.

▶ Contribute a weekly column in local newspaper to which experts contribute to readers' comments and suggestions.

▶ Establish a website: interactive discussion group for lay and health professionals.

▶ Key representatives of health authority trust or general practices become members of or attend community-based decision-making bodies in local politics, education, local authority, etc.

▶ Lay representative(s) or non-executive director(s) of trust, health authority, PCT interact with the boards of these organisations and the constituency and lay organisations they represent.

▶ Use a district or subdistrict-based information project to pool data held by the different organisations: for instance, the project might look at establishing the minimum amount of information required, and from which sources that information might be obtained, in order to carry out a health needs assessment for the topic in question. The sources will be diverse and are bound to include lay and health and social care organisations if a wide enough approach is taken. A shared lay–health professional lead will enable joint working to occur in a meaningful way.

or you want patients and the public to **receive** information about assessing and targeting patients' or the general public's needs from you

▶ Write for the local newspaper giving information directed at particular groups or informing the general public about particular groups.

▶ Local radio: health club type of health promotion programme such as 'smokebusters' aimed at engaging young people in stopping smoking.

▶ Target health promotion at hard-to-reach groups, through representatives of those groups acting as facilitators or different conduits such as touring theatre groups in schools performing a play highlighting health messages.

or you want patients and the public to **give** you information and advice about assessing and targeting patients' or the general public's needs

▶ Undertake a questionnaire survey: for example, a random selection from the local electoral register.

- ► Begin a poster campaign inviting people to write or phone in with comments and suggestions.
- ► Leave comment slips at public access points, day centres, pharmacies or playgroups, for instance, to reach people not using general practices.

*If your target population is an identifiable patient group or individual patients or carers within that group*

and you want to use an **interactive process for patients to give and receive** information and advice about assessing and targeting patients' or the general public's needs

- ► Meet with a patient participation group to discuss the issues, for them to act as go-betweens with the constituencies they represent, relaying concerns and ideas.
- ► Carry out a relevant research and development or audit project at local level in which health professionals and lay people or patients take active parts.
- ► Meet and confer with various special interest groups.

or you want patients to **receive** information and advice about assessing and targeting patients' or the general public's needs from you

- ► Contribute articles to local newsletters sent out to particular patient groups, for example users' group or carers' group newsletters, giving information known about needs and any mismatch in services.
- ► Welcome a representative of a particular group to the trust or general practice and arrange for them to observe evidence of need or best practice at first hand, to relay back to the populations they represent.
- ► Work through a friendly contact from a particular population group and get them to introduce you to their group for you to chat to them about the issues or employ a support worker as a link with that group of carers, the homeless, etc.

or you want patients to **give** you information and advice about assessing and targeting patients' or the general public's needs

- ► Run focus groups of hard-to-reach groups, user groups.
- ► Carry out interviews with consecutive individual patients who match the category under enquiry to find out more about their recent experiences, perceived needs (according to the patient) and observed needs (according to the health professional or an independent source). You might recruit subjects through the 'snowballing' technique whereby members of hard-to-reach groups who are known are asked to recruit others for the survey. You might use semistructured or unstructured interviews to encourage personal accounts.
- ► Give comment slips to people using the current service under review.
- ► Undertake a library search: there is a great deal of published literature about the needs of different population groups. Précis the material relevant to your locality.

▶ Set up a health parliament of a particular age group; for example, elected members of young people's groups and the education sector or older people from diverse groups with an older membership (sport, clubs, day centres, etc).

# Approximate costings of alternative methods of informing patients, involving patients and the public in planning and delivering healthcare

The costings are difficult to quantify because the exact budget will depend on the size of the exercise, how difficult it is to reach the target population, how skilled the personnel involved are or need to be, whether health professionals and others are incorporating the extra work into their daily activities and what the consequent opportunity costs are. Although the budgets look substantial when priced up in these approximate ways, the real costs of *not* involving the public or patients in meaningful ways could be very high, in terms of providing healthcare and services that are not in tune with what patients and the public need or will use or in human misery if patients are ill informed and poorly served.

## *Providing better education and information*

▶ Patient education leaflets, books, videos, audiocassettes: some non-promotional ones may be free from pharmaceutical companies or produced at subsidised rates. A practice library with sufficient material to lend to patients on a variety of conditions will cost at least £2000 with ongoing replacement costs if patients do not return the goods.

▶ One-off presentation and subsequent discussion: will take at least four hours of a health professional's time if preparation, travel and attendance are included.

▶ Writing an article for a local newspaper or a newsletter: depends on your skill and experience but it will probably take most health professionals about three hours to write and polish a 300-word article if they are unused to writing.

▶ Participate in a phone-in on radio: the time taken will include travel to and from the recording studio unless you speak on an outside phone line as a contributor to the discussion, rather than receiving and answering all the calls. Also remember to include the preparation time, as you would be unwise to speak on the radio without having reflected upon key points you want to bring up and having the basic facts or statistics to hand. Additional costs would be employing a member of staff on public relations duties if that was necessary to set up media and press contacts.

▶ Communication skills training: a training session should be as interactive as possible in a small group and may involve being videoed. This may entail a relatively expensive attendance fee unless the course is provided free as part of local professional training.

▶ Make your own video: your local university might have the facilities for you to make your own videos in a professional studio. The charges will depend on your local situation but might be about £1000 plus the costs of the videotapes.

▶ Your own web page: you can create your own web page through generally available software from an Internet access provider or pay someone with the know-how to design an attractive website for you and update it.

## Exchanging and obtaining information

▶ Focus group: staff time includes the facilitator's and observer's time for about two hours preparation, two hours attendance and several hours to write up a report, plus the secretarial time of about eight hours to transcribe a one-hour audiocassette tape and time to arrange the meeting. In addition, there are the costs of hospitality (maybe as much as a meal in a hotel), reimbursement of the participants' travel expenses and fees if applicable. The first time you run a focus group, you may need to buy a good tape-recording machine that picks up conversation from several metres away and a transcribing machine for the secretary. Costs for staff time alone might be £100–300 per focus group, depending on the seniority of staff employed on the exercise and the amount of preparation and writing-up time involved.

▶ A questionnaire survey or Delphi survey: one healthcare survey of 250 people, where the questionnaire was given out to respondents in person and returned in freepost envelopes, took 121 hours of a researcher's time from designing the questionnaires to writing up the report but excluding the preparatory stage of carrying out a literature search and gathering qualitative information by interviewing people typical of the population to which the questionnaire would later be despatched.[6] Other costs included the stationery, photocopying, postage, secretarial help with coding returned questionnaires (in the case cited, it took 27 hours) and a statistician's time for analysis (in this case, it took ten hours) and use of the computer hardware and statistical software. Thus, if an experienced research assistant with interviewing skills, earning around £10 an hour, was employed on the survey, the total costs might be around £2000 without taking account of overheads and expenses. As a guide for those who need to buy 'names' and their contact details from a population database for a survey, a typical cost might be in the region of £200 per 1000 randomly selected details from the electoral register of Stoke-on-Trent city (1999 prices).

▶ Undertaking an interview study: each interview of an hour probably takes about eight hours of the interviewer's time which includes preparing for the interview, making the appointment, travel, doing the interview, writing it up, with considerable extra time if the interviews are being taped and transcribed. Thus, a researcher earning around £10 an hour who spends about 400 hours carrying out about 30 interviews and extra time transcribing audiotapes will cost about £4000 plus travel costs and other survey costs such as statistical help if required.

▶ Rapid appraisal: in the project described on pp. 60–61, the GP author, a health visitor colleague and two others spent around 48 hours each actively gathering information.[7] There would be additional costs for preparing and writing up the interviews; the published report indicated that 25 or so interviews might be sufficient. If a researcher was used instead of health professionals and the researcher's time was priced at £10 per hour as in the other examples, the cost would be about £3200 for 25 transcribed interviews and, with around £2000 for gathering data from other sources, travel expenses and writing the final report, the minimum research bill would be about £5600 without overheads. There would be additional costs for the health professionals and other key figures to read, reflect on and discuss the findings and make plans to address the needs.

▶ Community development: programmes often have a community development worker employed as a full-time project worker on a temporary contract. The size and purpose of the project will dictate how long the community worker is employed for, and thus the costs, but such work often takes 1–2 years to gain the trust of the local community, build up networks, plan interventions and put them into place.

▶ Opinion poll: depends on the number of people being questioned and how accessible they are. If a market research company carries out such a survey, they charge commercial rates. You can get an idea of their charging rates from knowing that 'market research or similar organisations … charged approximately £4000 to £6000 (for recruiting jurors to a citizens' jury), a fee which included two group discussions with members of the public'.[8]

▶ Citizens' jury: typical costs are quoted as being around £16 000 plus considerable staff time,[8] up to £30 000.[9]

▶ Neighbourhood forum, patient participation group, user group: members are volunteers. Thus the expenses will be those of organising the event, possibly reimbursing travel expenses, providing light refreshments, taking minutes and writing and distributing any ensuing report or newsletter. Such a forum or group probably costs the NHS less than £100 a meeting, the comparatively low cost being because participants give their time without charge.

▶ Standing panel or health parliament: participants are volunteers. The costs include setting up the panel and recruiting members, organising the panel and obtaining new members to replace those whose term has expired or who have left the panel, communicating with the panel and enclosing a freepost means of response. If the clerical time required was about 12 hours a week and 500 participants took part in four polls a year, the costs might be around £6000 per year, plus overheads. However, one costing described by Staffordshire County Council for a citizens' panel in 1999, was £40 000 in the first year and £19 000 for the next two years[10] for four surveys a year organised by the London-based opinion poll firm MORI. The panel started with 200 citizens to which local borough councils could pose their own questions.

▶ Regular staff undertaking brief structured interviews of individual patients as part of consultations: these would have to be brief if they are to be incorporated into staff's normal work. Costs would be in training staff in interview skills and some clerical time to collate results.

▶ Nominal group: the organiser and facilitator might spend ten hours between them planning, organising and attending the group meeting and writing up a relatively brief report. The participants would probably be attending as part of their everyday work or as volunteers. Additional costs would be for the venue and hospitality and reimbursement of travel expenses. If the organising staff time was priced at £10 an hour as in the other examples given, the costs of running a nominal group would be less than £200 without taking account of the opportunity costs of any staff or lay participants.

## References

1 Department of Health (1998) *A First Class Service: quality in the new NHS.* Department of Health, London.

2 Roland M, Holden J and Campbell S (1999) *Quality Assessment for General Practice: supporting clinical governance in primary care groups.* National Primary Care Research and Development Centre, University of Manchester.

3 Rawaf S and Bahl V (1998) *Assessing Health Needs of People from Minority Ethnic Groups.* Royal College of Physicians, London.

4 Harris A (ed) (1997) *Needs to Know: a guide to needs assessment for primary care.* Churchill Livingstone, London.

5 Maxwell RJ (1984) Quality assessment in health. *BMJ.* **288**: 1470–2.

6 Chambers R (1993) How long did it take and what did it cost? A study of the time and costs involved in carrying out a research survey. *Postgrad Educ Gen Pract.* **4**: 37–40.

7 Murray SA, Tapson J, Turnbull L *et al.* (1994) Listening to local voices: adapting rapid appraisal to assess health and social needs in general practice. *BMJ.* **308**: 698–700.

8  McIver S (1998) *Healthy Debate? An Independent Evaluation of Citizens' Juries in Health Settings.* King's Fund, London.

9  Coote A (1999) Citizens' jury: a forum for health debate (editorial). *Update.* **18 March**: 485.

10  Manson R (1999) Families' chance to have say on council services. *The Sentinel.* **April 21**: 9.

# CHAPTER 7

# Giving patients and the public more information

## Informing patients and carers better

Patients ought to know what is wrong with them, what is likely to happen to them and what treatment they require. Why should anyone allow someone else to make decisions for them about their health? The better the information patients receive, the better able they are to participate in decision making about their own clinical management and make informed choices about different alternatives of care. There is some evidence that well-informed patients who actively share in making decisions about treatment have more favourable health outcomes – for instance, improved control of blood sugar levels in the care of diabetics.[1]

Giving patients more information has been associated with greater patient satisfaction,[2] as the study described in the box below shows.

> **Giving patients more information leads to increased patient satisfaction, better compliance and better recall and understanding of medical conditions[2]**
>
> A review of 41 research studies on this topic showed that there was a correlation between patients receiving good information at a health-care consultation and:
>
> ▶ greater patient satisfaction
> ▶ better compliance as measured by keeping future appointments or complying with their care regimen
> ▶ greater recall of how much information given at a previous consultation was remembered at a later visit
> ▶ greater understanding of the medical condition after the consultation
> ▶ patients being female
>
> *continued*

*continued*

and trends rather than correlations for whether patients received good information and their having higher levels of social class, income and educational attainment.

Patient satisfaction was increased according to the extent of communication in the consultation as rated by either the length of consultation in minutes or numbers of practitioner/patient utterances.

Some doctors and nurses are reluctant to share information, thinking that it may encourage patients to make more demands and so increase their workloads. Others fear that parting with information may render them more vulnerable to criticism if patients are in a better position to judge health professionals' performance and the standards of treatment they receive.

There may be a mismatch between what information doctors and other health professionals consider to be important and what patients think. The top three suggestions for a revamped Patient's Charter that members of the Patients' Association would like to see are that:

▶ general practitioners should have to give patients clear reasons before striking them off their lists
▶ patients should have access to data on their doctors' performance
▶ patients should be in charge of their own medical notes.

In a survey commissioned by Which, patients prioritised five areas of practice for improvement significantly more often than GPs did.[3] These were:

▶ the need to reduce time spent waiting – in the waiting room or for an appointment
▶ GPs' attention to what patients say
▶ GPs' explanations to patients
▶ convenience of surgery hours
▶ the extent to which GPs involve patients in treatment choices.

Another study of people's priorities with respect to general practice care found that patients the world over had many similar views, mostly focused on the quality of communication with their doctors.[4] The majority of respondents put most emphasis on being able to spend time talking with their general practitioners, doctors telling patients all they want to know about their illnesses, making patients feel free to talk about their problems and confidentiality of information about patients.

If carers are better informed and their contribution to the overall care of the dependent person is acknowledged, welcomed and respected by health professionals, they should be able to take more responsibility and be more likely to seek professional help appropriately.

▼

**Patient empowerment.**

Giving patients more and better information is more complex than it may seem at first sight. Doctors and other health professionals are more likely to favour some patients with information above others. A study undertaken in America showed that well-educated, middle-aged female patients were the group most likely to receive good information at their healthcare consultations.[5] The findings are reported in the box overleaf.

> **Patients' characteristics can compromise the effectiveness of interpersonal care**
>
> Doctors are less likely to involve certain types of patients in making decisions about their healthcare than others.[5] Patients who seem to have the least interaction with their doctors are:
>
> ► elderly people aged 75 years and older
> ► young adults, aged under 30
> ► patients who did not attend further education
> ► patients from minority groups
> ► male patients.
>
> Men were less likely to participate in decision making if they were consulting male doctors than if they were seeing female doctors and participated less than women patients consulting doctors of either gender, in this American study.

## What information do people want?

The Consumers' Association has recently called for the establishment of a single central and impartial source of information on medicines and treatment, so that the public is well informed about health issues.[6] People want 'real' information so that they know:

► what services are available, at practice or district levels, and how to access them
► how to make the best use of the services or facilities available
► what quality and quantity of services they are entitled to
► whether standards of care or service provision are being met
► what the options are for treating their condition – medical or social management, complementary or traditional therapy, invasive or conservative treatments or no treatment
► what the risks are for having, and not having, different treatments
► what the outcomes and side effects of treatment might be
► how to prevent a medical problem becoming worse, recurring or occurring in the first place
► what to expect whilst a treatment is being carried out and how they will feel
► what they can do to help themselves or the person they are caring for.

**Good information is key to patient empowerment**[7]

Users' Voices relays patients' views about mental health services at seven sites. The report emphasises the importance of providing good information to those with mental health problems and its recommendations can be generalised to other groups of people using the health service. The project was developed by the Sainsbury Centre for Mental Health using interviewers who were themselves service users. The majority of those they interviewed had severe and enduring mental health problems and were on medication. About half of the patients interviewed did not think that they were getting enough information and thus felt that they were recipients of mental health care, rather than being involved in decision making about their management. The report concludes that all prescriptions for psychotropic medication should provide full information about the benefits and side effects of the drugs. Community mental health teams should develop central indexed stores of information concerning community resources, benefits, housing, work projects, and advocacy. All staff should have a basic knowledge about this information which should be available in all the locally spoken languages and in forms accessible to those with sensory impairments. There should be user involvement in planning and delivering individual care for the purpose of empowerment rather than compliance.

So if you review the standards of information being given to patients and the general public by the colleagues with whom you work, you will need to:

1 find out from patients what information they want – you cannot assume that those who provide healthcare know what information people require
2 identify subgroups of your patient or general public populations with particular information needs and think at the same time of the best ways to meet their needs. Would written or audio material suit them best or will it mean appointing someone to give out information personally face to face or via a telephone helpline?
3 review the quality of information patients are receiving; map out what is happening at present. Look to see how much of the literature or information available is out of date and if it is written or spoken at the right level for people's needs or understanding. Ask people if they found it useful and how the information might be improved
4 monitor that patients or the public receive the information that is available, especially hard-to-reach groups.

# Informing the general public, including non-users of NHS services

Giving non-users information about services may make them more aware of how they might access healthcare, what is available and when it is appropriate for them to seek medical advice or help.

Informing the general public about health issues and the constraints on the NHS should enable them to share in decision making about allocating or rationing resources between competing services and between particular groups of people in the population. The open and accountable culture expected of the NHS includes sharing information with patients about costs and performance in the NHS. The increased emphasis on openness might encourage clinicians to become more candid too and tell patients what they really think about people who continue to gain weight, lie about having given up smoking or continue with a self-defeating lifestyle whilst taking antidepressant treatment!

# Communicating information

Practices, trusts and health authorities should be reviewing their communication strategies to provide the quality and quantity of information individuals or the public at large want. This will include:

▶ mapping out information requirements, including understanding staff's and patients' different perspectives

▶ communication skills training for individual practitioners to improve their ability to involve patients in decision making about their own care, explain risks, give information at the right level for a particular patient's needs or understanding and determine their preferences

▶ structural changes to ensure that practitioners have ready access to electronic sources of reliable clinical information and guidelines, with the option of being able to print out associated patient information material (for example, decision support programmes). Medical libraries should be linked in

▶ direct access to reliable information for patients and the general public at large, for instance through practice-based libraries, telephone helplines or recommending particular Internet sites for lay people

▶ effective and appropriate information technology and computer skills training for all NHS staff

▶ the pooling of information relating to the determinants of health in respect of the local community held by the many health and social care organisations and local authority departments, so that practices, trusts and health authorities have access to relevant socioeconomic and other health data for their populations

▶ improving the sharing of medical information about individual patients on a 'need-to-know' basis; this will include topics such as who has rights of personal and electronic access to medical records, shared care patient-held records, informed consent, confidentiality issues

▶ maintaining continuity of care and consistency of health messages with the increasing emphasis on multiprofessional working

▶ working with the media and press: briefing them proactively to get positive messages across and minimise negative or hostile reporting

▶ a steering group to oversee communication, for example with liaison groups to explain difficult issues at the interface between the NHS and media, or work with local communities; to co-ordinate the strategic objectives and work programme; and look after the dissemination of information to the target groups

▶ finding the resources to implement the communication strategy.

## Telephone helplines

The three examples in the box show how hungry the general public is for basic information. Helplines could be a cost-effective option for practices, trusts or health authorities to consider.

---

**Telephone helplines – how popular are they and what information do they provide?**

▶ A healthline in North Staffordshire takes on average 14 telephone calls per day from the general public. The service is staffed for six hours every weekday, with an answerphone for the rest of the time. A resource centre has been developed with literature and videos available to the public on loan. The most common information provided is about the availability of health services in the area (41% of callers) with 8% of callers wanting information about self-help and support groups, 2% about waiting times, 5% about Patient's Charter rights and standards, 6% advice about lifestyle and 18% information about diseases or medical conditions; 20% want advice on various other topics. The healthline staff welcome callers in person as well.

▶ A freephone national helpline for a hayfever treatment giving information about the day's pollen count attracted 55 000 calls in 1993.[8]

▶ A telephone helpline set up to give advice about arthritis after a television programme on the topic received 650 calls, mainly from women aged 50–70 years old.[9] Most wanted advice about pain control; concern about medication and side effects were common queries too.

## Patient information leaflets

Leaflets are one way of providing patients with clear and easily understood information. Have a look at all the information leaflets in your cupboards at work and see if they:

▶ are easy to read, free of jargon and use straightforward text
▶ capture the reader's interest
▶ are relevant for: your setting, population, usual approach
▶ offer varied advice for: different age groups, reading ability, people with particular needs
▶ are up to date with information about evidence or best practice
▶ are accurate: messages are clear and not misleading
▶ give full details of all treatment alternatives, rather than being partisan and favouring a particular option (especially if supplied free from a commercial source)
▶ give balanced views about options, risks, side effects, uncertainties of investigation or treatment
▶ maintain a positive tone to encourage action and change behaviour for the better.

You could make your own leaflets: get your visiting physiotherapist or dietician to jot down their top tips and photocopy them. But it would be easier to use a standard electronic database from which you can print off your own leaflets. You can run copies off with the patient present and always be sure that patients are getting current literature, so long as your CD-ROM source is up to date. Some of the electronic packages that are available are given in the Appendix.

The more interactive or visual the material you distribute to inform patients, the more likely it is to be successful in increasing the patient's understanding of the issue or the condition and engaging them in changing their behaviour. The kinds of ideas in circulation are:

▶ symptom diaries for patients to make regular records
▶ enrolling the patient on a register to receive regular mailings of information relating to a health condition or disease
▶ videos with associated information booklets for patients to log how their own symptoms and feelings compare
▶ pictorial representation of comparative risks of treatment
▶ checklists and quizzes to get patients relating the information to themselves or as screening tools looking for previously unrecognised health problems
▶ credit type cards for requesting priority appointments at the surgery (for example, given out in advance to adolescents in case they require emergency contraception or for people with severe mental health problems).

> **Public participation in action**[10]
>
> Tameside and Glossop Primary Care Trust have developed a mission to 'INFORM, EDUCATE and INVOLVE the public, patients, carers and staff in health related issues'. They have evolved a comprehensive programme of public involvement that includes a range of community education and learning projects and activities, such as:
>
> ▶ West Pennine healthy schools scheme: enabling local primary and secondary schools to promote exercise and drama within the umbrella of promoting health
> ▶ exercise programme and lifestyle group for adults classified as obese
> ▶ promoting positive aspects of the cultural, educational and health promotion elements of healthy living to local Asians
> ▶ educating members of the local Mind Centre about healthy eating
> ▶ providing young people with better knowledge and understanding of available health services
> ▶ a newsletter for the over 50s living locally about the quality of health and social care services to encourage their contribution to monitoring the quality of services received and provide information.

## Patient's Charters

Patient's Charters may empower patients by publishing standards against which to measure the care and services that are available to them. But they cannot be successful if the published standards of care are unrealistic because of resource constraints and disappointed patients are frustrated by not receiving the care or services to which they were led to believe they were entitled. More could be made of the potential for charters to be used to publicise patients' responsibilities and help to control unnecessary demands on the NHS.

## Communicating via the media

The local media are cheap and effective ways for practices, trusts and strategic health authorities to get information across to the local population. It is important for those working in the NHS to build up good relationships with individual editors, producers and journalists so that reports of successful initiatives and new developments are widely broadcast. You should be proactive and feed information to the media whilst the stories are current. The 'good' news will keep the local community informed and help to counterbalance the not-so-good articles and stories.

There will be times when the developments planned by practices, trusts and health authorities will be unpopular with the local community as care is shifted into the community or centralised to bigger hospitals, local units are closed and vulnerable people moved to live in community-based housing. If services are discontinued because of financial constraints or to make way for new services, the people who were receiving them may use a public protest to try to force continuation of the services. You should anticipate problems ahead and contact the media before the bad news breaks or the local community starts a campaign about unpopular decisions to discharge vulnerable people into the community. Brief the media with detailed information about the health issues or the funding constraints. Undertake pre-emptive work to explain about equality and that discrimination against particular subgroups of the population is unacceptable. Just as you should recognise the importance of involving lay people at an early stage in planning changes to NHS services, so you should engage with the media unless there are good reasons for regarding the information as being too sensitive for release into the public domain.

If you do speak on the radio, remember to be well prepared.

- Find out more about the programme and the person who will be interviewing you, whether it will be a straightforward interview or if the presenter usually tries to catch people out.
- Write down a few key points or 'sound bites' that you want to say at sometime in the interview.
- Write down the name of the presenter or other people involved so that you can use them.
- Use simple words, avoid jargon and speak clearly.
- Sit still and maintain the same distance from the microphone so that your voice sounds steady and confident.
- Write down any basic facts or statistics in case someone asks you; you might not remember in the heat of the moment.
- Try to sound friendly and relaxed and imagine you are just talking to a friend instead of a microphone.

If you write an article for the local press:

- write in the usual style of the newspaper
- use simple words, short sentences and short paragraphs
- avoid jargon and complicated arguments
- give accurate information
- place your key points at the beginning of the paragraphs
- keep to the pre-agreed word count
- make an opening statement that will capture the reader's interest
- don't expect to be paid for the article necessarily, just be glad of the opportunity to get your views or messages across
- submit your article on time in line with the agreed deadline.

▼

**Make sure you have the basic facts at your fingertips if you agree to speak on the radio.**

## References

1 Kaplan SH, Greenfield S and Ware JE (1989) Assessing the effects of physician–patient interactions on the outcomes of chronic disease. *Med Care.* **33**(12): S110–27.

2 Hall JA, Roter DL and Katz NR (1988) Meta-analysis of correlates of provider behavior in medical encounters. *Med Care.* **26**(7): 657–75.

3 Which (1992) GPs, your verdict. *Which.* **April**: 202–5.

4 Grol R, Wensing M, Mainz J *et al.* (1999) Patients' priorities with respect to general practice care: an international comparison. *Fam Pract.* **16**(1): 4–11.

5 Kaplan SH, Gandek B, Greenfield S *et al.* (1995) Patients' and visit characteristics related to physicians' participatory decision-making style. *Med Care.* **33**(12): 1176–87.

6 Consumers' Association (2003) *Patient Information: what's the prognosis?* Consumers' Association, London.

7 Rose D (2001) *Users' Voices.* The Sainsbury Centre for Mental Health, London.

8   Dyke P (1994) Freephone telephone numbers: what role will they play in patient/doctor information? *Med Dialogue*. **March**: 1–4.

9   Scott D (1994) Patient information: is this the way forward? *Med Dialogue*. **January**: 1–4.

10  Curtis G (chair) (2003) Public Participation in Action. Thameside and Glossop Primary Care Trust, Manchester.

# ▶ APPENDIX

# Health information for health professionals, patients and the public

## Useful organisations

**Benefits Agency**
To find your local benefits agency office use http://www.dwp.gov.uk/localoffice/index.asp. For general information on benefits use http://www.dwp.gov.uk/index.asp

**Carers UK**
This is the leading organisation for carers, helping them to speak with a stronger voice. Website: www.carersonline.org.uk. See also www.carers.gov.uk and http://members.benchmarking.gov.uk

**Centre for Health Information Quality**
The Centre acts as a source of expertise and knowledge for the NHS and patient representative groups on all aspects of patient information, to improve the NHS's capability, competence and capacity to provide good, evidence-based patient information.
*Contact*: Centre for Health Information Quality, Highcroft, Romsey Road, Winchester, SO22 5DH. Tel: 01962 872264. Fax: 01962 849079. Website: www.hfht.org/chiq/

**Charity Commission**
There are three regional offices covering England and Wales:

London: Harmsworth House, 13–15 Bouverie Street, London EC4Y 8DP. Tel: 0870 333 0123. Fax: 020 7674 2300.

Taunton: Woodfield House, Tangier, Taunton, Somerset TA1 4BL. Tel: 0870 333 0123. Fax: 01823 345003.

Liverpool: 20 Kings Parade, Queens Dock, Liverpool L3 4DQ. Tel: 0870 333 0123. Fax: 0151 703 1555.

Website: www.charity-commission.gov.uk

### Citizens Advice Bureaux (CABs)

CABs give free, confidential, impartial and independent advice on subjects such as benefits, debt, housing, legal matters, employment, immigration and consumer issues. To find your nearest CAB, search the CAB directory www.citizensadvice.org.uk or for advice: www.adviceguide.org.uk

Or write to: National Association of Citizens Advice Bureaux, Myddelton House, 115–123 Pentonville Road, London N1 9LZ. They have a useful advice search directory: http://www.nacab.org.uk/cabdir.ihtml

### Cochrane Collaboration Consumer Network

The Consumer Network is a consumer organisation within the Cochrane Collaboration that supports and develops consumer participation in the Collaboration, by identifying important questions from the point of view of people who train consumers to help hunt out trials, get involved in commenting on drafts of Cochrane reviews, or spreading the results of Cochrane reviews in their communities. Membership of the Consumer Network is free of charge and is intended for people who are really interested in getting involved in the organisation. Website: www.cochraneconsumer.com

### College of Health

The College of Health is a national charity founded to represent the interests of patients. The College publishes a range of reports, guidelines and packs based on independent research.

*Contact*: Publications Unit, College of Health, St Margaret's House, 21 Old Ford Road, London E2 9PL. Tel: 0208 983 1225. Fax: 0208 983 1553. Email: info@collegeofhealth.org.uk. Website: www.collegeofhealth.org.uk

### Commission for patient and public involvement in health

The purpose of this commission is to promote the involvement of the public in decisions affecting local NHS services. Further information can be obtained from http://www.doh.gov.uk/involvingpatients and http://www.doh.gov.uk/patientadviceandliaisonservices

### Communities for Health

The Communities for Health initiative brings together a coalition of organisations and projects that aim to support people to play active roles in planning and implementing action. This is co-ordinated by the Health Voice Network. Website: http://www.communitiesforhealth.net/

### Community Health Exchange (CHEX)

CHEX is part of the Scottish Community Development Centre (SCDC) and aims to promote and support best practice in community development approaches in challenging health inequalities throughout Scotland. Website: http://www.scdc.org.uk/chex/

### Consent

The Department of Health website outlines good practice and guidance for obtaining consent for research and treatment. Website: http://www.doh.gov.uk/consent/index.htm and http://www.doh.gov.uk/consent/twelvekeypts.htm. See the following websites for more details of seeking consent with particular groups:

► older people http://www.doh.gov.uk/consent/olderpeople.pdf
► people with learning disabilities http://www.doh.gov.uk/consent/learningdisability.pdf
► children http://www.doh.gov.uk/consent/childrensguidance.pdf
► prisoners http://www.doh.gov.uk/prisonhealth/seekingconsentin prison.pdf

### Consumers in research

Consumers in research are a group set up to advise the NHS on how best to involve consumers in research and to ensure consumer involvement improves the way research is prioritised, undertaken and disseminated in the NHS.

*Contact*: Consumers in NHS Research Support Unit, Wessex House, Upper Market Street, Eastleigh, Hampshire, SO50 9FD. Tel: 023 8065 1088. Email: admin@conres.co.uk. Website: http://www.conres.co.uk/index.htm

### Creative Spaces

Creative Spaces is about creative community involvement in urban design. It aims to present inclusive, holistic and creative approaches which are particularly successful at involving communities previously difficult to reach. Website: www.creativespaces.org.uk/

### Democratic Health Network

This subscription-based network provides policy advice, information, research and a forum for the exchange of good practice between local government and health. Website: www.dhn.org.uk

### Department of Health

Publishes various documents and circulars on patient and public involvement. Website: www.doh.gov.uk/involvingpatients

### Department of Work and Pensions

The Department of Work and Pensions (DWP) provides an A–Z of benefits and services. Website: http://www.dwp.gov.uk/lifeevent/benefits/index.asp

### DIPEx

DIPEx is an Oxford-based charity that has a website based on in-depth research studies of patients' experiences of health and illness. It links video, audio, and written interviews with evidence-based

information about the health problem and possible treatment options. Besides offering support for patients and their carers and friends, it provides a patient-centred perspective to researchers, managers, health professionals and those who commission health services. So far they have detailed information on hypertension, colorectal cancer, prostate cancer, testicular cancer, breast cancer and cervical cancer and cervical screening, with lots more modules expected soon.
*Contact*: DIPEx, Department of Primary Health Care, Institute of Health Sciences, University of Oxford, Old Road, Headington, Oxford OX3 7LF. Tel: 01865 226672. Email: info@dipex.org. Website: www.dipex.org

## Expert Patients Programme

Self-management training programmes for patients with chronic diseases, run by the NHS in England. Programmes were originally piloted in 26 sites and are now being implemented by trusts.
For further information on the Expert Patients programme visit the *Our Healthier Nation* website at www.ohn.gov.uk/ohn/people/expert.htm

## Folk.us

Folk.us supports and encourages professionals to involve service users, disabled people and carers in research.
*Contact*: School of Psychology, Washington Singer Building, University of Exeter, Perry Road, Exeter EX4 4QG. Tel: 01392 264 660. Email: folk.us@ex.ac.uk. Website: http://latis.ex.ac.uk/folk.us/findex.htm

## Health for All

Health for All is an internationally recognised structure which enables those working to improve the health of local communities and apply Health for All principles, to meet and share information, research and experiences. Website: http://independent.livjm.ac.uk/healthforall/

## Health Promotion Information Centre

The HPIC has a series of health-related databases for health professionals on specific population groups: young people, older people, black and minority ethnic groups and people with learning disabilities. The databases include up-to-date information about nationally available resources that promote health and healthy living. The databases can be accessed via a search requested through HPIC. Tel: 0207 413 1995. Fax: 0207 413 2605. Email: healthpromis@hda-online.org.uk. Website: http://healthpromis.hda-online.org.uk

## Health Voice Network

The Health Voice Network (HVN) is co-ordinated by the Hub and Spokespeople Project, which is managed by UK Health for All Network and funded by the Department of Health. The HVN aims to enable people to have more of a say in planning and improving services that affect their health by sharing their experiences, ideas, knowledge, questions and skills. Membership is open to all and includes staff, individual service users, members of the public, community groups and organisations who provide advocacy, campaigning, education, finance, information, training and other resources to support people to get involved in planning services.

*Contact*: Hub and Spokespeople Project, Health for All Network (UK) Ltd, New Century House, 52–56 Tithebarn Street, Liverpool L2 2SR. Tel: 0151 231 4283. Fax: 0151 231 4209. Email: admin@healthvoice-uk.net. Website: http://www.healthvoice-uk.net/

### Help for Health Trust

The Trust aims to provide people with the information they need to make healthy choices. It produces databases of consumer health information and has a specialist health information research unit.

*Contact*: Help for Health Trust, Highcroft, Romsey Road, Winchester, SO22 5DH. Tel: 01962 849100. Fax: 01962 849079. Website: www.hfht.org/

### Housing Corporation Bank of Good Practice

Includes references to good practice in involving residents. Website: www.housingcorp.gov.uk/resources/bgp.htm

### Hub and Spokespeople Project

The Hub and Spokespeople Project managed by the UK Health for All Network and funded by the Department of Health aims to improve people's health by enabling them to influence policies and services that affect their health. They also co-ordinate the Health Voice Network.

*Contact*: Hub and Spokespeople Project, Health for All Network (UK) Ltd, New Century House, 52–56 Tithebarn Street, Liverpool L2 2SR. Tel: 0151 231 4284. Fax: 0151 231 4209. Email: A.Boyd@livjm.ac.uk. Website: http://independent.livjm.ac.uk/healthforall/hubspoke/main.htm

### Involving People Team

Their role is to implement Patient Focus and Public Involvement. As part of the work of the team a National Network has been established which consists of members of the public as well as NHS Scotland staff. The team has also developed a toolkit of approaches to involve people – the Building Strong Foundations Toolkit – and are currently preparing a newsletter which will provide updates on the work of the team and examples of good practice from across Scotland. Website: www.scotland.gov.uk/library3/health/pfpi-00.asp

### King's Fund

The King's Fund is an independent health charity that promotes the health of people in London through policy analysis and development and information about health and social care. It has five major programmes of policy and development work: community care, effective practice, health systems, primary care and public health, and key themes include promoting cultural diversity, tackling health inequalities and developing public involvement.

*Contact*: King's Fund, 11–13 Cavendish Square, London W1G 0AN. Tel: 0207 307 2400. Website: www.kingsfund.org.uk

### Mental Health Foundation
Provides summary information on many user involvement resources. Website: www.mentalhealth.org.uk

### Modernisation Agency
The NHS Modernisation Agency has produced a booklet for project leaders on patient involvement, which has a number of references/ contacts and examples of recent practice. The guide can be accessed at www.modern.nhs.uk/improvementguides

### National Association of Councils for Voluntary Services (NACVS)
NACVS have a directory of local Councils for Voluntary Services.
*Contact*: NACVS, 177 Arundel Street, Sheffield S1 2NU. Tel: 0114 278 6636. Fax: 0114 278 7004. Email: nacvs@nacvs.org.uk. Website: www.nacvs.org.uk

### National Association for Patient Participation (NAPP)
NAPP is a charity that provides support and encouragement for the formation of Patient Participation Groups in primary care. Affiliation to the national network of groups is available to new and established groups. Website: www.napp.org.uk

### NHS Clinical Governance Support Team
Patient and public involvement is at the centre of clinical governance in the Clinical Governance Support Team (CGST). Patients help the CGST to shape their programmes of work through continuous dialogue and partnership working. Their take on patient involvement is: respecting patients as people, including patients/the public as team members, and creating power with (not power over) patients and the public.

*Contact*: NHS Clinical Governance Support Team, 2nd Floor, St John's House, 30 East Street, Leicester LE1 6NB. Tel: 0116 295 2000. Helpline: 0116 295 2074. Email: support@ncgst.nhs.uk. Website: www.cgsupport.org

### National Council for Voluntary Organisations (NCVO)
Regent's Wharf, 8 All Saints Street, London N1 9RL. Tel: 020 7713 6161. Helpdesk: 0800 2798 798. Email: ncvo@ncvo-vol.org.uk. Website: www.ncvo-vol.org.uk

**National electronic Library for Health**
Includes the electronic library for patient, user, carer and public involvement in health and social care. NeL-INVOLVE is part of the National electronic Library for Health (NeLH) and aims to establish a new 'special collection' of best available useful information on user involvement, within NeLH. A pilot site is being established and will cover the following areas: patient and public involvement in policy and service; research and development; patients as partners in their own care; patients' rights; consumer involvement in research; patients as teachers. Website: www.nelh.nhs.uk

**NHS Centre for Reviews and Dissemination (CRD)**
The Centre provides the NHS with information on the effectiveness and cost-effectiveness of treatments and the delivery and organisation of healthcare. It aims to disseminate research to the medical profession, nurses, midwives, health visitors and allied health professionals.
*Contact*: NHS Centre for Reviews and Dissemination, University of York, York, YO10 5DD. Tel: 01904 433634 (general enquiries), 01904 433707 (information service), 01904 433648 (publications). Email: crd@york.ac.uk. Website: www.york.ac.uk/inst/crd/

**Patients' Association**
The Patients' Association is an independent charity pressing for the involvement of patients as full partners in decision making at all levels. Website: www.patients-association.com

**Patients' Forum**
Provides information for member organisations who represent the interests of people who use health services, to enable them to strengthen their work in informing and influencing decision makers. Website: www.thepatientsforum.org.uk

**Plymouth Health Impact Assessment (HIA)**
Aims to develop community-based HIA capacity, resources and tool-kits, so that community groups can use HIA to improve local health and increase their influence with decision makers. Website: www.plymhealthimpact.co.uk

**Portal for Patients' Advice and Liaison Services (PALS)**
Portal for PALS provides easy access to relevant information about PALS, such as government guidance, Patients' Voice and a guide to the NHS. Website: http://www.nelh.nhs.uk/pals/

**Quest Trust**
The Quest Trust aims to support local activists in improving the quality of life in their communities by enabling people to share information and ideas about successful economic and social regeneration

effectively, in particular to promote and encourage resident-led, local solutions. Website: www.quest-net.org

### Research for Communication and Public Involvement (RCPI)

The RCPI website features research and experience based information for improving communication and public involvement in large organisations. Website: http://www.wpi.org/rcpi/

### Royal College of General Practitioners

College publications and other patient-centred literature are available from the Sales Office.
*Contact*: Sales Office, Royal College of General Practitioners, 14 Princes Gate, Hyde Park, London SW7 1PU. Tel: 0207 823 9698. Fax: 0207 225 0629. Email: sales@rcgp.org.uk. Website: www.rcgp.org.uk

### Sainsbury Centre for Mental Health

Their website includes publications on user involvement. Website: www.scmh.org.uk

### Scottish Association of Health Councils

24A Palmerston Place, Edinburgh EH12 5AL. Tel: 0131 220 4101. Website: www.show.scot.nhs.uk/sahc/

### Standing Conference for Community Development (SCCD)

SCCD is a UK-wide membership organisation which aims to be a strong voice for community development, through supporting people who support communities. SCCD brings together practitioners, policy makers, researchers, local authorities, academics, non-profit organisations and grass roots workers throughout the UK. Website: www.sccd.org.uk

### Telephone Helplines Association

A search facility of over 1000 helplines in the UK. Tel: 0845 120 3767. Website: http://www.helplines.org.uk/

### The Prince of Wales's Foundation for Integrated Health

The key principles of the Foundation are based on a holistic and integrated approach to healthcare which include an emphasis on the importance of individuals taking more responsibility for their own healthcare, and good access to the treatment approach of their choice. *Contact*: 12 Chillingworth Road, London N7 8QL. Tel: 020 7619 6140. Fax: 020 7700 8434. Email: info@fihealth.org. Website: www.fihealth.org

# Useful material for patients, managers and health professionals

**Anderson W, Florin D, Gillam S, Mountford L (2002)** *Every Voice Counts. Primary care organisations and public involvement.* King's Fund, London.

**Ask the Patient series, User Involvement, Consumer Audit, Primary Health Care, Rationing, Disabled People:** many reports and guidelines in these topics published by the College of Health (see above for contact details).

**College of Health (1994)** *Consumer Audit Guidelines.* College of Health, London. A guide to College of Health Consumer Audit methods including interviews, focus groups and observation, with practical examples, case studies, sample topic guides and letters, etc.

**Consumers in NHS Research Support Unit**
Publishes guidance on the different levels of consumer involvement and how consumers can be involved in different stages of research. Also publishes guidance for researchers. For details of publications contact: Consumers in NHS Research Support Unit, Wessex House, Upper Market Street, Eastleigh, Hampshire SO50 9FD. Tel: 02380 651088. Email: admin@conres.co.uk
These are also downloadable from the website: www.conres.co.uk

**Coulter A, Entwistle V, Gilbert D (1998)** *Informing Patients: An Assessment of the Quality of Patient Information Materials.* King's Fund, ISBN 185717 214 0. Much existing patient information material is out of date, inaccurate and misleading. The book demonstrates how the NHS can improve material to help patients share in decision making about their treatments from an informed standpoint (see above for contact details).

**Department of Health catalogue of free publications and information**
The catalogue aims to provide an up-to-date index of all publicity material in an easy-to-follow guide. To order the catalogue and free publications write to: Department of Health, PO Box 410, Wetherby, LS23 7EN or fax 0990 210 266. Website: www.doh.gov.uk/publications

**eMIMS**
This CD-ROM is a prescribing information package designed for GPs. It includes pictures of every tablet or capsule, patient information leaflets, prescribing notes on diseases and videos.

*Contact*: Haymarket Medical Limited, 174 Hammersmith Road, London W6 7JP. Tel: 0208 267 4681. Fax: 0208 267 4681. Email: emims@haynet.com. Also on Internet: www.emims.net

**Fletcher G, Bradburn J (2001)** *Voices in Action Resource Book: training and support for user representatives in the health service.* College of Health, London. The book is designed to equip health service users to work in active partnership with health professionals to improve NHS services.

**Gaskin K (1997)** *How to Work with Your Doctor.* Royal College of General Practitioners, London (see above for contact details).

**Getting involved in research: a guide for consumers**
An excellent guide to the questions all users should ask before becoming involved. http://www.conres.co.uk/pdf/guide_for_consumers.pdf

**Glossary of Acronyms**
Glossary of Acronyms also provides a collection of legal materials used in health and social services. Website: www.sochealth.co.uk/glossary/glossary.htm
These are also well covered in The NHS Confederation (2002) *The Pocket Guide to the NHS in England/Wales/Scotland* (alternative versions). NHS Confederation, London.

**Guide to Paying Consumers Actively Involved in Research**
This is a non-prescriptive guide that outlines the principles of good practice in paying consumers who are actively involved as partners in health and social care research. It includes guidance on expenses, time, expertise and sets out examples of rates. Website: www.conres.co.uk/pdf/guide_to_paying_consumers110302.pdf

**Help Groups and Support Organisations** is a comprehensive guide to over 800 British self-help groups and support organisations. *Contact*: G-Text, Freepost NWW6775, Blackpool, FY4 3GA. Email: g-text@blackpool.net. Website: www.blackpool.net/www/g-text/

**Kelson M (1997)** *User involvement: A practical guide to developing effective user involvement strategies.* College of Health, London. Guidance on how to involve health service users in the planning, monitoring and development of health services. Available from www.collegeofhealth.org.uk

**Kelson M (1998)** *Promoting Patient Involvement in Clinical Audit.* College of Health, London. A report designed to help those responsible for developing ways of promoting the effective, active and appropriate involvement of patients in clinical audit activity. It considers why, who, when and how to involve patients in clinical audit activity, providing real examples.

**Kelson M (1999)** *Involving Older People in Local Clinical Audit Activity.* College of Health, London. The focus of this booklet is on securing more active participation by older people in audit.

**Kelson M (1999)** *Patient-Defined Outcomes.* College of Health, London. A report prepared for the Clinical Outcomes Group Patient Subgroup looking at involving patients in all aspects of outcomes work.

**Kohner N, Leftwich A (1998)** *Partnerships: A Training Pack: training for partnerships with patients and clients.* Health Development Partnerships, CoH and NHS Executive, London. Designed to help healthcare professionals work on their skills for partnership with patients and clients. Covers work on users' experiences and needs, self-awareness and attitudes, communication skills, interpersonal skills, relationships with patients and clients, choice and decision making and ethical dilemmas.

**McIver S (1993)** *Obtaining the Views of Health Service Users about the Quality of Information.* King's Fund, London (see above for contact details).

**Olszewski D, Jones L (1998)** *Putting People in the Picture.* Scottish Association of Health Councils, Edinburgh (see above for contact details).

**Patient Pictures**
Range of books containing clinical drawings for use by doctors and nurses when describing medical conditions and treatments to their patients, covering basic anatomy, disease progress, investigations and treatments. Available from the Sales Office, Royal College of General Practitioners (see above for contact details).

**PhysioTools**
Produce CDs for GPs to make their own patient information leaflets on home care for stroke patients and incontinence.
*Contact*: PhysioTools UK, on 01749 890870. Website: www. physiotools.com

**Rose D (ed) (2001)** *Users' Voices. The perspectives of mental health service users on community and hospital care.* The Sainsbury Centre for Mental Health, London.

**RTFB Publishing**
Provide customised patient education materials for health authorities and PCTs, including booklets, leaflets and audiocassettes.

*Contact*: RTFB Publishing Ltd, Building 2, Shamrock Quay, Southampton, SO14 5QL. Tel: 02380 229041. Fax: 02380 227274. Website: www.whatshouldido.com

**Signposts – *A Practical Guide To Public And Patient Involvement In Wales***
The purpose of the guide is to provide advice in carrying out a baseline assessment of arrangements for public involvement; guidance underpinning the production of annual plans; examples of best practice in public involvement; and in-depth information about how to undertake public involvement in a range of different circumstances. It is free on the web. Website: http://www.wales.gov.uk/subihealth/content/nhs/signposts/index.htm

**Smarter Partnerships**
Smarter Partnerships is a toolkit to assist local authorities and their partners to improve partnership skills and performance. Website: www.lgpartnerships.com

# Patient support groups

**Arthritis**
Arthritis care: 18 Stephenson Way, London NW1 2HD. Tel: 020 7380 6500 (general enquiries); 0808 800 4050 (helpline); Website: www.arthritiscare.org.uk

**Asthma**
National Asthma Campaign: Providence House, Providence Place, London, N1 0NT. Tel: 020 7226 2260 (office); 0845 701 0203 (helpline). Website: www.asthma.org.uk

**Cancer**
CancerBACUP: 3 Bath Place, Rivington Street, London, EC2A 3JR. Tel: 020 7696 9003 (general enquiries); 0808 800 1234 (helpline). Website: www.cancerbacup.org.uk

Macmillan Cancer Relief: 89 Albert Embankment, London, SE1 7UQ. Tel: 020 7840 7840 (office); 0808 808 2020 (helpline). Website: www.macmillan.org.uk

**Children with Disabilities**
Contact a Family: 209–211 City Road, London, EC1V 1JN. Tel: 020 7608 8700 (office); 0808 808 3555 (helpline). Website: www.cafamily.org.uk

## Depression

Depression Alliance: 35 Westminster Bridge Road, London, SE1 7JB. Tel: 020 7633 0557. Website: www.depressionalliance.org

Samaritans: The Upper Mill, Kingston Road, Ewell, Surrey, KT17 2AF. Helpline: 08457 909090; 020 8394 8300. Website: www.samaritans.org.uk

Cruse Bereavement Care: Cruse House, 126 Sheen Road, Richmond, Surrey, TW9 1UR. Helpline: 0870 167 1677. Tel: 020 8939 9530. Website: www.crusebereavementcare.org.uk

## Diabetes

Diabetes UK: 10 Parkway, London, NW1 7AA. Tel: 020 7424 1000 (office); 020 7424 1030 (careline). Website: www.diabetes.org.uk

## Eating Disorders

Eating Disorders Association: 103 Prince of Wales Road, Norwich, NR1 1DW. Tel: 0870 770 3256 (office); 0845 634 1414 (adult helpline); 0845 634 7650 (helpline – youth link). Website: www.edauk.com

## Elderly

Age Concern England: Astral House, 1268 London Road, Norbury, London, SW16 4ER. Tel: 020 876 57200 (office); 0800 009966 (information line). Website: www.ageconcern.org.uk

Help the Aged: 207–221 Pentonville Road, London, N1 9UZ. Tel: 020 7278 1114. Website: www.helptheaged.org.uk

Alzheimer's Society: Gordon House, 10 Greencoat Place, London SW1P 1PH. Tel: 020 7306 0606; 0845 300 0336 (helpline). Website: www.alzheimers.org.uk

## Eyesight

RNIB: 105 Judd Street, London, WC1H 6NE. Tel: 020 7388 1266 (office); 0845 766 9999. Website: www.rnib.org.uk

SENSE: 11–13 Clifton Terrace, Finsbury Park, London, N4 3SR. Tel: 020 7272 7774. Website: www.sense.org.uk

## Family Planning

British Pregnancy Advisory Service: Head Office: Austy Manor, Wootton Wawen, Solihull, West Midlands, B95 6BX. Tel: 08457 304030 (helpline). Website: www.bpas.org

Family Planning Association: 2–12 Pentonville Road, London, N1 9FP. Tel: 020 7837 5432 (office); 0845 310 1334 (helpline). Website: www.fpa.org.uk

## Heart Disease

British Heart Foundation: 14 Fitzhardinge Street, London, W1H 6DH. Tel: 020 7935 0185. Information line: 08450 708070. Website: www.bhf.org.uk

## Migraine

Migraine Action Association: Unit 6, Oakley Hay Lodge Business Park, Great Folds Road, Great Oakley, Northamptonshire, NN18 9AS. Tel: 01536 461333. Website: www.migraine.org.uk

Migraine Trust: 45 Great Ormond Street, London, WC1N 3HZ. Tel: 020 7831 4818. Website: www.migrainetrust.org

## Skin

Acne Support: PO Box 9, Newquay, TR9 6WG. Tel: 0870 870 2263. Website: www.stopspots.org

National Eczema Society: Hill House, Highgate Hill, London, N19 5NA. Tel: 0870 241 3604 (helpline); 020 7281 3553 (office). Website: www.eczema.org

Psoriasis Association: Milton House, 7 Milton Street, Northampton, NN2 7JG. Tel: 0845 676 0076. Website: psoriasis-association.org.uk

Vitiligo Society: 125 Kennington Road, London, SE11 6SF. Tel: 020 7840 0855 (office). Website: www.vitiligosociety.org.uk

Herpes Virus Association: 41 North Road, London, N7 9DP. Tel: 020 7607 9661 (office); 020 7609 9061 (helpline). Website: www.herpes.org.uk

## Smoking

Quit: Ground Floor, 211 Old Street, London, EC1V 9NR. Tel: 0800 002200 (quitline); 020 7251 1551 (office). Website: www.quit.org.uk

## Special Conditions

Association for Spina Bifida and Hydrocephalus: ASBAH House, 42 Park Road, Peterborough, PE1 2UQ. Tel: 01733 555988. Website: www.asbah.org

Down's Syndrome Association: 155 Mitcham Road, London, SW17 9PG. Tel: 020 8682 4001. Website: www.dsa-uk.com

National Association for Colitis and Crohn's Disease: 4 Beaumont House, Sutton Road, St Albans, Hertfordshire, AL1 5HH. Tel: 01727 830038 (office); 0845 130 2233 (helpline). Website: www.nacc.org.uk

National Autistic Society: 393 City Road, London, EC1V 1NG. Tel: 020 7833 2299. Website: www.nas.org.uk

National Reye's Syndrome Foundation: 15 Nicholas Gardens, Pyrford, Woking, Surrey, GU22 8SD. Tel: 01932 346843. Website: www.reyessyndrome.co.uk

# Useful British websites

**AIDS/HIV : Terrence Higgins Trust**
http://www.tht.org.uk/

**Alzheimer's Society**
http://www.alzheimers.org.uk

**Asthma and Allergy Research**
http://www.users.globalnet.co.uk/~aair/

**Cancer Help**
http://www.cancerhelp.org.uk

**Dental phobics information**
http://www.dentalfear.org/

**Diabetes: adults**
http://www.diabetes.org.uk/; www.diabetes-insight.info

**Digestive Disorders**
http://www.digestivedisorders.org.uk

**Disabled Living Foundation**
www.dlf.org.uk

**Epilepsy**
http://www.epilepsy.org.uk/

**Hepatitis Network**
http://www.hepnet.com/

**Institute of Psychiatry**
http://www.iop.kcl.ac.uk/iop/home.shtml

**Marie Stopes Institute**
http://www.mariestopes.org.uk/

**Mental Health Foundation**
http://www.mentalhealth.org.uk/

**Multiple sclerosis**
http://www.mssociety.org.uk/

**Prostate Help Association**
http://www.u-net.com/~pha/

**Spina bifida and hydrocephalus**
http://www.asbah.org

**Twins and Multiple Births Association**
http://www.tamba.org.uk

**Women's health: infertility**
http://www.womens-health.co.uk/infertility.htm

# Media – useful contacts

### Association of Broadcasting Doctors

Publishes a regular newsletter updating members about advances in medicine and news of the profession, about which they might broadcast or write.

*Contact*: Jackie Petts, Association of Broadcasting Doctors, PO Box 15, Sindalthorpe House, Ely, Cambridge CB7 4SG. Tel: 01353 688 456. Fax: 01353 688451. Website: www.broadcasting-doctor.org

### Media Medics

Nationwide network of medical writers and broadcasters.

*Contact*: Media Medics, Deben House, Chapel Row, Woodham Ferrers, Essex CM3 8RN. Tel: 01245 328062. Website: www.media-medics.co.uk

### The Society of Medical Writers

Has a regular journal and database of authors with areas of interest and expertise. Editors commission articles from the database. GPs, health professionals and others with an interest in health may join as members. Has twice-yearly residential meetings and a regular newsletter.

*Contact*: The General Secretary, Society of Medical Writers, 633 Liverpool Road, Southport, Merseyside PR8 3NG. Tel: 01704 577839. Website: www.somw.org

### Tim Albert Training to Improve Your Writing Skills

One-day public courses on effective writing, writing scientific papers and setting up newsletters. Run courses in London or for in-house groups elsewhere.

*Contact*: Paper Mews Court, 284 High Street, Dorking, Surrey RH4 1QT. Tel: 01306 877993. Email: tatraining@compuserve.com. Website: www.timalbert.co.uk

# ► INDEX